OMWG

Oh, My Wonderful God!

A Tribute in Verse to Our Lord and Savior

Diane Fritz Yeo

ISBN 978-1-0980-8455-4 (paperback)
ISBN 978-1-0980-8456-1 (digital)

Christian Faith Publishing, Inc.
832 Park Avenue
Meadville, PA 16335
www.christianfaithpublishing.com

Printed in the United States of America

Dedicated to my grandchildren:
Anika Marie,
Gunnar Eugene,
Andrew Joseph,
Bridger Eugene,
and
Elijah Stephen

O God, You have taught me from my youth,
And to this day I declare Your glorious wonders.
Now also when I am old and gray-headed,
O God do not forsake me,
until I declare Your strength to this generation,
Your power to everyone who is to come.
(Psalm 71:17–18)

My son, give attention to my words;
incline your ear to my sayings.
Do not let them depart from your eyes;
keep them in the midst of your heart;
for they are life to those who find them,
and health to all their flesh.
(Proverbs 4:20–22)

Preface

The year is 1948 in the beautiful farmland of rural South Dakota.

Picture in your mind a large two-story farmhouse built in the 1920s, with a country porch on the front side and on that porch a wooden swing moving in the breeze.

Now step into the living room, where there is a maroon sofa covered with a protective chenille bedspread that would only be removed before company came. Picture a three-year-old girl beside that sofa, head bowed, eyes closed, hands folded, kneeling beside her mother.

This little girl was me shortly after my mother discovered there was a more personal way to know our Savior besides just the knowledge of His existence two thousand years ago. She was concerned that I, too, know this Jesus early in life, and so I followed her instruction to ask Jesus to come into my heart and life.

At that time, I became His and He became mine. Of course there was much more to take place—a whole life to live with maturing in my faith, correcting misconceptions, facing everyday trials and temptations, sins needing to be confessed and forgiven, learning from studying on my own as well as from other Christians.

This learning is still ongoing because I am still a work in progress. But through it all, I am His and He is mine.

Now fast-forward to just a few years ago, the time when my husband's parents and mine had all passed on to glory. I began to contemplate how fragile life is and how generations pass and are soon forgotten. It was then that I decided I wanted to leave some sort of legacy, something written that would tell my grandchildren, great-grandchildren, and even generations to follow that there is a loving, living God who desires a relationship with them, and that this grandmother was (and still is) His and He is mine!

I also wanted them to dig into His Word to discover for themselves how interesting, meaningful, and complete it is!

One day, as I was reading, I came across Psalm 71:17–18. I know I have read the Psalms before, but never had this verse come alive to me until just this moment, just when I needed a confirmation to what I was thinking. Here it is: "O God, You have taught me from my youth. And to this day I declare Your glorious wonders. Now also when I am old and gray-headed, do not forsake me until I declare Your strength to this generation, Your power to everyone who is to come."

And so I began to write a poem. I started with who God is and who He is to me, and then I decided I had to tell about the fall of man and then, of course, God's plan before the foundations of earth, to send His Son to redeem and reestablish us with our loving Creator.

So I had to tell of His chosen people through whom Jesus would come, following them down through the Scriptures and, well, you've got the picture—I just kept writing!

Let me tell you of our triune God,
the Father of mercy and love,
His Son, our Savior, Jesus Christ,
And His Spirit, the power from above.   *John 14:16*

God created me with an awareness of Him   *Romans 1:19–20*
and placed eternity in my heart.   *Ecclesiastes 3:11*
His greatness I cannot comprehend; for God
is eternal—without beginning or end!   *Psalm 102:27*
I have found Him to be my great
shepherd and friend;   *Exodus 33:17*
He knows me and calls me by name.   *John 10:3*
He is holy and just, the giver of life,   *Hebrews 13:8*
Immutable—forever the same!   *Psalm 102:27*

In the beginning God laid the   *Genesis 1–5*
foundations of earth.
The Heavens are the work of His hand.   *Hebrews 1:10*
All living things that move and breathe
Were created just as He planned.
God said, "Let's make man in our own image
and put him in a place of great beauty."
To tend and to keep this great Garden of Eden
Was man's God-given duty.
To assure that man would not be alone,
God designed Eve from Adam's rib bone.

A mind to choose, a heart to love, a soul to give,   *Mark 12:30*
And strength to act—all were bestowed upon man.
Would these gifts be used to give God glory?
Sadly not—let me tell you the rest of the story.

God gave them only one special command.
When the tempter came, could
they take a firm stand?
"Good versus evil is best left unknown,
So, the fruit of that tree, you must leave alone.
If you eat of that tree, you will surely die—
Fruit from all others I do not deny."

Into the garden the serpent came, Satan,
the devil, all one and the same.
In all of his deceitfulness, he fed them a lie,
"If you disobey God, you won't surely die!"

They listened, they took, their
innocence disappeared,
They hid from their God whom they now feared!
Sin and death entered the world
with a very high cost:
All creation would suffer; man
was spiritually lost!   Romans 8:20–22

God clothed them with garments
made from animal skin,
The first blood was shed because of their sin.
They were expelled from the garden—
sent to live out their curse. Estranged
from God! What could be worse?

After man's sin, God could react in two ways:
Total destruction to end our days,
Or a plan of redemption could be set into motion—
this He would choose to show His devotion.
You see, in eternity, before our time began,
Our Triune God had made a plan!   1 Peter 1:20
The serpent might well have deceived God's
creation, but God's plan included a chosen nation.
Through them His Offspring
would crush Satan's hold—
Redemption! Life Eternal! The
greatest story ever told!
And so it is, even today—
We think we know better; we want our own way.
During our life here on earth we are given a choice:
Will we believe God's truth or the scheming voice?
Jesus came to save, not condemn;   John 3:17
through His blood we are blameless!
Amen and amen!   Ephesians 1:4

To Adam and Eve two sons were born;
Cain worked the soil; Abel kept flocks.
When offerings were made to God, Abel's
lamb was accepted, Cain's produce was not.
God spoke to Cain giving him another chance,
"If you do what's right, won't you be accepted?"
But sin became Cain's master as
God's warning he rejected.
In great anger he murdered Abel; all
humanity would be affected.
When Eve gave birth to Seth, she credited
God for a son to take Abel's place.
Through Seth's descendants hope dawned
for the future of the human race.

***

But as generations passed, evil   Genesis 6–11
permeated the earth;
more murders occurred—life had little worth.
Man's choices were not as they should be.
Nothing but violence was there to see.
God finally said, "Only one
man still walks with me!"
To Noah He spoke, "Build an ark of wood,
I'll save your family, for you live as you should.
Build it just as I say and take animals aboard;
Ignore man's rebuke for I AM the Lord.
All other life will perish as flood
waters rise, Man's wickedness on
earth has caused his demise."   Hebrews 11:7

Noah listened and did as God instructed.
Questions were asked as the ark was constructed.
Noah preached of the righteousness and justice
of his God, but men scoffed at what he said.
Having no faith, they were oblivious
to the destruction that lied ahead.
To all God's commands Noah had complied.
As God sealed the doors, there was safety inside.

For forty days and forty nights
water flooded the land;
Yet the ark and all therein were
saved by God's own hand!
As the waters receded and the earth became dry,
God set a rainbow of color across the sky.
"This rainbow is my covenant sign. Never
again will waters destroy all mankind!
Be fruitful and multiply and again fill the earth;
I'll bless this land with new life—rebirth!"

Man had heard God's command; but their
rebellious nature made a new plan:
"Let's stay in one place and become well-
known by building a tower to the sky!"
They'd do it their own way; God's
command they'd defy,
But God was there to foil their plan; He
confused their language—oh foolish man!
So, from Noah's sons nations were birthed,
then scattered by God to cover the earth.

***

In God's own time He began His plan   Genesis 12–21
to find a nation and select a man.
Abram, from Haran, was the man
of God's choice. Imagine his shock
when he heard God's voice!
Abram had only experienced a culture that
worshiped many gods—gods made of stone.
So imagine his reaction when the One and
Only God spoke out to him alone!
He might have thought, "A god who
speaks—how can this be?
And what could he want from a man like me?"

God spoke, "Leave your people, your
present life, and your land, I have a future
for you far beyond what you've planned."
Follow Me and I will make your name great;
through you the whole world will be blessed;
Your offspring shall number as the sands of the
sea; have faith; I AM! I'll give you the best!"

By faith Abram followed; his journey had begun;
God would bless him and test
him before it was done.
Abram relied on himself when
difficulties arose, as they must.
But God intervened as He
taught Abram to trust.

To Abram and wife Sarai God promised a son.
Impossible! Sarai's childbearing-years were done!
The promise of an heir, they
could not understand,
So Abram took matters into his own hand!
Sarai offered her servant Hagar to
bear Abram a son. Ishmael was born;
family conflict had begun!
Eventually Hagar and Ishmael would be sent
away, but their lives would not come to an end.
For God had heard their cries and promised
from them a great nation would descend!

God was patient and faithful in
His relationship to this man.
He continued to remind Abram
of His sovereign plan.
God made a covenant with Abram and
gave him a new name. Abraham, meaning
"the father of multitudes," he became.
God's covenant with Abraham was
sealed in Abraham's own skin.
The rite of circumcision was extended
to every male of his kin.

When Abraham had reached the land of
Canaan, his nephew Lot, who had come with
him too, chose to settle on the plains toward
the East. Its lush and fertile land he did view.
But the sinful cities of Sodom and
Gomorrah corrupted this beautiful land.
God could not tolerate their wickedness;
judgment would fall from His hand!
Because of God's love and commitment
to Abraham, His plan of destruction
to him was revealed.
Abraham interceded for his nephew Lot,
and God listened as Abraham appealed.
Lot and two daughters escaped as fire
and brimstone fell from the skies.
But Lot's wife became a pillar of salt when
she looked back with regret in her eyes!

***

When Abraham was 100 and Sarah
90 years old, their son Isaac was
born, just as they had been told.
They had underestimated just what God can do;
Isaac was proof; God's promises were true!

***

On a mountain called Moriah   Genesis 22–32
Abraham's greatest test would be
God's instruction: "Let your son Isaac
be the sacrifice you offer me!"
Abraham's faith was steady. He did not falter.
He took Isaac with him to prepare the altar.
God said, "Abraham, Abraham, I now see that
you have not withheld your son from me.
I'll provide the lamb; set your son free!"

This story is difficult for us to understand!
God wanted the complete trust
from His servant Abraham.
God desired Abraham's unfailing faith in
His Sovereignty—faith beyond sight, faith
that knew God would set Isaac free!   *2 Corinthians 5:7*
Abraham's faith <u>*was*</u> *proven strong; he*
trusted his God could do no wrong!   *Hebrews 11*
This was also God's picture of what He would
do as He offered His Son for me and you.
Jesus would leave the heavens above,
enter humanity to show God's love.   *John 3:16*
He'd bear the shame of death on a cross;
willing to do this, He'd suffer our loss.
But in victory over sin and the grave, Jesus
was resurrected with the power to save!

***

From Isaac came Esau and Jacob, his brother
the latter was to replace the other.
Esau valued not his birthright, and his
father's blessing was not received.
By trickery Jacob was given the blessing,
which could not be retrieved.
Father Isaac, who was blind, didn't
realize he was being deceived.
So extreme was Esau's anger
that Jacob had to flee
But an encounter with God at Bethel
told Jacob who he was to be.

Jacob married Leah and Rachel
and fathered twelve sons;
the twelve tribes of Israel had now begun.
But God was not through
preparing Jacob for his plan;
On his journey Jacob wrestled
with God's own Man!
As he wrestled with God, Jacob would not
let God go until God's name, His nature,
and His blessings, Jacob would know.
After this event, Jacob's life was not the same;
God blessed him and said, "Israel
will be your new name!"

God's promise continued from generation
to generation; the Israelites were
preserved to be His called nation.
"I called you into righteousness
and I will hold your hand,   *Isaiah 42:6*
I will keep you and yet give you, do you understand?
You'll show to all, my covenant; to the
nations a light you'll be; to open blind
eyes and to set prisoners free!"

***

Jacob favored his son Joseph   Genesis 37–40
and gave him a coat.
Joseph's dreams of his dominance
caused him to gloat,
"You'll all bow to me; my dreams do reveal."
His brothers hated him and made a deal
with Midianite traders passing by;
Joseph was sold into slavery; their evil
act covered with a lie! Joseph was taken
to Egypt, many trials to face.
But his ability to interpret Pharaoh's
dreams found him grace.
"There is no man as wise and discerning as you.
Over my household and all of Egypt
you'll reign; you'll be number two!"
So from an Egyptian prison, Joseph
rose to a man with great power.
God had planned to use Joseph
for this special hour.

Acting on the dream that the Pharaoh had had,
Joseph stored up grain in years-of-
plenty for the famine would be bad!
Over the face of the earth the famine spread.
Countries far and near bought grain
from Joseph and were fed.
Included was Joseph's family,
who also was in need;
they came bowing down before
him seeking help indeed!
Joseph's dream of long ago had
come to realization.
God had used the brothers' hateful
act to save many from starvation!

This is how our God was and still is today;   *Romans 8:28*
He works all things for good in His own way.   *Ephesians 1:11*
Evil instigated by the enemy
Is changed to fit God's will—that's sovereignty!

In Joseph we see a picture of Christ's story told;
rejected by His brethren, He also was sold.
He faced trial and was deserted
after false accusation.
On the cross He shed His blood, resulting
in sin and death's nullification.
But He arose, offering abundant life
in place of spiritual starvation!

***

God's wisdom and sovereignty   Job
can best be expressed
through God's servant Job, who
Satan put to the test.
Through trials far worse than
most humans endure,
Job's confidence in his God remained secure.
Perplexed by the reasons for his
suffering, Job still said,
"Though God slay me, yet I'll trust
Him; vindication lies ahead!"
Friends came to Job with their own theology,
their reasons for his distress and pain.
But their words were found to be inadequate;
the ways of God they could not explain,

God spoke to Job through the whirlwind—
His omnipotence was unveiled loud and clear.
Job's mind was enlightened by
the greatness of his Lord,
As God's words fell upon his ear.
Without knowledge, Job had spoken
of things he did not comprehend.
Trying in his humanity, himself to defend.
He had trusted in what he had heard about
God, but now his eyes had been made to see
That God's ways are greater than any
man's knowledge of God could ever be!
Job's prayer: "I now repent in ashes and dust.
You, oh Lord, can do everything;
in You I put my trust!"

In the words of Job:
"What will I do when God confronts me?
What will I answer when called to account?"
Without the blood of my precious Savior,
my fears would begin to mount!
Throughout most of our lives we've
been similar to Job—
obscuring God's counsel without proper knowledge,
questioning things we can't understand.   *1 Corinthians*
Things we now see through a glass dimly lit,   *13:9–10, 12*
We'll someday envision as glorious and grand!
On that day, the whole earth
will be full of His glory;
Then we will know the climax of His story!

***

When the Israelite nation grew   Exodus 1–4
in numbers and might,
The new King of Egypt was
afraid they'd take flight.
He set taskmasters over them.
Bondage was their lot.
To kill all Israel's baby boys was his evil plot!

But God saw their situation; He
had plans for their freedom.
When the time was right, He'd
provide a man to lead them.
A baby in a basket, Pharaoh's daughter did find.
He was rescued from death; he was
Moses, the leader God had in mind!

Though raised in the Egyptian palace,
Moses saw his people's plight;
As a young man and in his own
strength, he was willing to fight!
But God had a better plan for Moses
to help set His people free.
It came to Moses after years spent
in Midian, and more maturity.

From a fiery bush the voice of God spoke,
"I have seen my people and heard their cry;
You, Moses, will request their freedom,
which Pharaoh will deny.
But with My signs and wonders, he will agree,
and with a great miracle I'll set my people free!"
"Not me, Lord! I'm not that
eloquent," was Moses reply.
God's answer: "I Am who I Am; words
and strength I will supply!"

God gave Moses signs to perform
using God's miraculous power.
With these, he'd show his people that
he was God's man for this hour.
When Moses still requested that
God choose another,
God appointed a spokesman for
him—Aaron, his brother.

Pharaoh's heart was hardened;   Exodus 5–12
he refused to let them go.
The Israelites were worried; this
just added to their woe.
The plagues God had sent had not
changed Pharaoh's mind—
Not until the Passover blood, the
prophetic plague God designed.

Blood from the Passover Lamb on
the doorposts was placed;
When the Angel of Death passed, the
Israelites received God's grace.
But all the firstborn in Egypt were struck dead.
"Rise, go out from among us!" Pharaoh said.

Far in the future Jesus would be   *John 1:29*
the Passover Lamb to set mankind free.
With His life-giving blood, He'd wash sin away
For those who believe, there would
be freedom that day!

***

So God led His people in the wilderness way,   Exodus 13–16
with fire at night and a cloud by day.
But by the time they reached the Red Sea,
Pharaoh had changed his mind; he had pursued
them, and his chariots were not far behind.

The children of Israel walked on dry land in the midst of the Red Sea.

The people said to Moses, "Did
we come here to die?"
The Lord spoke to Moses, "Why do you cry?
Lift your rod up; stretch it over the sea.
The waters shall part; on dry land you will flee!"
So the Lord saved Israel from the enemy's hand,
And all knew He was Lord—
God of sky, sea, and land!
Then Moses and the Israelites
sang a song to the Lord.
Their enemy had been defeated
without their lifting a sword!
"Oh, Lord, our strength, our
salvation and strong tower;
You are awesome in glory, holiness, and power.
With Your unfailing love and
Your mighty Right Hand,
You will lead us on to the Promised Land!"

On their journey through the desert,
God rained manna from the sky;
fresh meat in the evening He did supply.
Sometimes the people grumbled about the
rules of God's provisions; Moses relied on
His God as he made many decisions.

One day on Mt. Sinai God called to His servant: Exodus 19–23
"Moses, speak to the people;
this is what you must say,
'On eagles' wings I carried you bringing
you to this day. Now as My treasured
possession, a nation so holy, you must
keep my covenant and obey me fully.'"

Moses prepared his people, telling
them all God had said.
Cleansed and consecrated, the Israelites
to the mountain's base were led.
There was thunder and lightning, the
mountain violently trembled!
Fear struck the hearts of those assembled.
The Lord descended in fire and
with a billow of smoke,
He called Moses to the top and with him spoke.
"I am the Lord your God; no other
gods shall you have before Me.
To no other thing in heaven above or
earth beneath shall you bow your knee.
Take not the name of your God in vain.
Six days shall you labor; but the Sabbath
is holy—from your work refrain.
Honor your father and mother that
you may have a long life span.
Do not murder, commit adultery,
lie, steal, or covet any man."

Other laws of guidance and protection
God gave them to obey.
He promised His angel would
guide them on their way.

They offered burnt offerings; blood
was sprinkled on each head.
From the Book of the Covenant, Moses read,
"This is the blood of the covenant
the Lord has made with you."
The people responded, "Everything we will do."
God's first covenant of law with
animal's blood was sealed.   Hebrews 9:20
When Jesus died and shed His blood, God's
new covenant of grace was revealed!
No sins are forgiven without blood being
shed—this was according to law.   *Hebrews*
But the Messiah came to offer Himself; through   *10:9–10*
His blood we are redeemed once for all!

On Mt. Sinai, for forty days and nights, Moses   Exodus 31–34
received instruction of all that God had planned.
He returned with the tablets of stone on which
the laws had been written by God's own hand.
The people had grown impatient, and forgetting
their promises to God, they melted all their gold.
They formed a calf and worshiped its image—
completely against what they'd been told.
God's anger was aroused; so quickly they
had turned aside from what He'd declared!
Moses, in anger, broke the tablets of stone but
interceded for them, asking that they'd be spared.
Those who chose the calf over their Holy
God were slain, and Moses offered a prayer
of atonement for those who did remain.
The Lord blotted from His book those
who had sinned against Him.
Then He said, "Now go lead the people
to the place I have intended for them."
Moses requested that God's presence go with
him as he continued to shepherd the flock.
God showed Moses His glory as He kept
him hidden safely in the cleft of a rock.
God wrote on stone tablets what He had
written before. *(A God of second chances is He!)*
And Moses returned to his people,
his face shining with the glory of
God, for all his people to see!

***

A tabernacle in which God would
dwell was built at His request.
God's words: "My presence will go
with you, and I will give you rest."
The Tabernacle, its furnishings, the Arc   Exodus 40
and Mercy Seat were prepared as God
instructed; each detail was complete.
A cloud hovered over as God's
glory filled His place.
A cloud by day and fire by night was
to assure them of His grace.
If the cloud was taken up, they
would journey on their way.
But if it remained, it was a sign for them to stay.

God sustained His people as they began their
journey in the wilderness; they delighted in the
prosperity with which their God did bless.
But at times they disobeyed; their
hearts were turned away.
Moses was there to remind them,
"Choose God. He's Life!
But you'll perish if you stray!

From the mountains of the Amorites,   Deuteronomy
the Promised Land was now in view.   1–29
Moses said, "Look! Go possess this
land that our God has given you!"
After sending in spies to scout out the land,
they were afraid to obey their God's command.
They cried, "God brought us out of
Egypt to fall into the Amorites' hand!"
Because of their rebellion, they
had to face God's penalty.
None except Caleb and Joshua, the
Promised Land would ever see.

So back to the wilderness for forty years
they were led, until all the unbelieving
generation who disobeyed were dead.
Moses followed God's guidance as
they wandered these years.
His reteaching of God's Law fell
on the young listening ears.
"You shall love the Lord your God with
all your heart, soul, and strength."
Moses continued to stress their
obedience to God at length.

Right before the Israelite nation   Deuteronomy
reached their promised destination   30–34
Moses gave a final blessing to all.
On Joshua, a man of great wisdom,
the mantle of leadership did fall.
God's promise was given: Joshua 1–10
"Be courageous and strong; do
not fear nor be afraid.
Your God goes with you each step you
take. He'll never leave you nor forsake."

31

Along with this promise, instructions were
given necessary for Joshua's impending success.
If he followed these commands from his
God, the Promised Land he would possess:
"The Book of the Law shall not depart from you;
on it you must meditate day and night.
Observe all that is written therein and your
way will prosper as you begin the fight."

*The Word of God in its entirety
has been given to us today.*   2 Timothy 2:15
*Our instructions are the same if it
is to guide us on life's way.
We must study God's Word, meditate on its
meaning, and apply what it says as we act.*   2 Timothy 3:16
*When false doctrines arise, we'll be able to
discern what is heresy versus what is fact.*   Ephesians 4:14

With Joshua as their leader, they
crossed over the Jordan
and possessed the Promised Land.
Because Joshua was strong in faith and
committed to God, the Canaanites
were given into his hand.
This was not an easy task; much wisdom
and boldness were required.
As Joshua acted on God's instructions,
many miracles transpired.

As the ark approached the Jordan,
the waters stopped flowing; they
crossed over on dry ground.
God used Rahab, the harlot, to hide the spies,
so by the enemy they couldn't be found.
The commander of the Lord's army appeared
to Joshua and instructed him of God's ways.
The city of Jericho would be conquered after
they marched around its walls for seven days.
As the trumpets sounded, the people
shouted and the walls crumbled to dust.
Only Rahab and her family were saved because
in Israel's God she had put her trust.

Israel, led by Joshua, continued the conquest
of many heathen lands. During one of the
battles Joshua gave a ridiculous command:
"O, sun stand still; O moon stop!"
(*The Israelites must have thought
he'd gone over the top!*)
But the sun did stop, and it delayed
going down for an entire day.
Fighting for Israel God listened to a
man—God had done it Joshua's way!

God had fulfilled all He had promised   Joshua 21–24
to their fathers long ago.
With His continual guidance, they
had defeated many a foe!
As each tribe was allotted their portion of
land, they would experience a time of rest.
Joshua spoke seriously with them as
he gave his farewell address.
"This day is a day of decision. Choose
to fear the Lord and serve Him with all
sincerity of heart, or choose to serve the
gods your fathers served from the start.
But as for me and my house,
we will serve the Lord!"
The people all agreed and gave him their word.
A covenant was written; to this
promise they'd all comply.
A stone became their witness lest
their God they would deny.

The people of Israel served the Lord
their God during all of Joshua's days.
They had seen what God had done for them
and acknowledged His mighty ways.
But the next generation knew not the
Lord; their memory of His works did fail.
Straying from His covenant, they served
other Gods—the Ashtoreths and Baal!
This can be a lesson today for all
who love and serve their Lord.
Pass on your Christian heritage, for
this He commands in His word.

"Impress God's commandments upon
your children both night and day.   *Deuteronomy*
Talk about them in your home and   *6:6–9*
as you walk along the way.
Write them on your doorposts and also on your gate.
So to this God you love and worship,
the next generation will relate!

The new generation's sinful ways   Judges 2–7
God could not tolerate.
Enemy nations were allowed to subdue
them in order to set them straight.
Yet in their time of trouble when
they cried up to heaven,
God was faithful to forgive them
even seventy times seven!   Matthew 18:22

The Lord raised up judges to help
free them from bondage and restore
them to prosperous days.
But alas, they were only "temporary saviors," for
the people reverted to their unfaithful ways.

During the time of the judges
when Israel fell into sin,
they were conquered by the Canaanites,
whose king was named Jabin.
With nine hundred chariots of iron,
so powerful was he, the Israelites knew
without God's help there'd be no victory.

They cried out to the Lord; in His
mercy He heard their plea.
He used Deborah, Israel's judge at that
time, to speak words of prophecy:
She called on Barak to lead Israel's army;
to him she gave the Lord's command,
"Deploy 10,000 troops to meet Jabin's army,
and I will deliver them into your hand."
So, on that day in the presence of
Israel, Canaan was subdued.
Praises were sung to their mighty Lord—
thankfulness was their mood.

After forty years Israel did evil in the
sight of the Lord once again.
So God allowed the hand of the
Midianites to prevail against them.
So impoverished were they by the Midianites'
actions, they cried out to their Lord once more.
The Angel of the Lord appeared to Gideon—
God would work through a man as before.

"The Lord is with you, mighty man of
valor!" To Gideon this was a new insight!
But Gideon questioned Israel's circumstances
and why this was their plight.
The Lord continued, "Have not I sent you
with My power? The battle will be My fight!"
Gideon destroyed the altar of Baal,
replacing it with one to his Lord.
This angered the enemy armies as
they gathered up their swords!

Gideon, still cowering in fear, asked
God for one more confirming sign;
God met his request and reassured
him, "This battle will be mine!
The number of warriors must be only a few.
Israel will recognize what I, their God, can do!"

At night, three hundred valiant men using
torches as their lamps, surrounded the
enemy army on every side of the camp.
With their trumpets blasting they shouted,
"The sword of the Lord and Gideon!"
The enemy panicked, turned against each
other, and that was the defeat of Midian!

***

Again, Israel acted unfaithfully
in God's holy sight.
And again, deliverance into the hand of
the Philistines was their awful plight!
But God planned for a man by whom
the Philistines would be defeated.
God's providence over Israel
was once more repeated.

The Angel of the Lord appeared   Judges 13–16
to Manoah and his wife
with the promise of the birth of a
child and instructions for his life.
Samson was to be set apart for God's
service, to take the vow of a Nazirite.
God, through the Holy Spirit, would bestow
on him great physical power and might!

As Samson grew, the Lord stirred his
heart to confront the Philistines.
He'd use the strength given him to
defeat them by unusual means.
When the power of the Spirit came upon him,
Samson killed a lion with his bare hands.
In retaliation to a Philistine wager gone
wrong, He set on fire all their crop lands.
The ropes with which he was tied fell with
ease as he exerted his strength once again;
And with the jawbone of a donkey he
struck down one thousand men.

The enemy feared this mighty man
with his extraordinary power.
They sought to discover the secret of his
strength hour after hour. Samson's demise was
his relationship with a woman called Delilah.
She pestered him daily to know his
secret till he finally said, "I'll tell ya!
No razor has ever been used on my
head. I'm a Nazirite from birth!
My strength lies in my tresses—if cut,
I'd be like any man on earth!"

While Samson slept, Delilah called for a
man to cut off his magnificent locks.
Without strength, he was subdued by the
Philistines, blinded, and put into stocks!
The Philistine rulers assembled, sacrificing
to their god and proclaiming victory!
But God heard Samson as he prayed,
"Oh, Lord, remember me!
Just once more, O God, may I
avenge myself and thee!"
So God strengthened Samson one
more time, answering his plea.
As he took hold of the temple pillars,
his strength returned again.
The temple fell killing Samson, the rulers
and lords, and all the Philistines therein!

***

In the book of Ruth, we learn of a   Ruth 1–4
Moabite woman, whose love and faith in
God gave her a place in God's plan.
Elimelech, Naomi his wife, and two sons moved
to Moab because of a famine in Bethlehem.
But not too long afterward, Elimelech and
both sons died, leaving Naomi with only
her two daughters-in-law by her side.

Naomi planned to return to
Bethlehem, her home.
But Ruth, her daughter-in-law, was
determined she not return alone.
She insisted, "Entreat me not to leave or
turn back from following you! Wherever
it is that you will go, I will go too!
Your people will be my people, and
your God will also be mine!"
Her love and devotion to Naomi
was a love of God's design.

Elimelech's relative named Boaz was in his
field, as it was Bethlehem's harvest season.
"If I show I will work, this man may
take notice," Ruth began to reason.
So Ruth worked in the field of Boaz, gleaning
what did remain. Hoping that he would
take note and his favor she might gain.

When Boaz saw Ruth, he inquired about
her, "To whom does this woman belong?"
He was told she came with Naomi from Moab
and had worked in the fields all day long!
Boaz then spoke to her, asking
her to follow his direction,
"My daughter, glean along with all the other
young women and be assured of my protection."
Why Boaz would be so kind to her, Ruth
questioned, as she could not understand
how he would treat so compassionately
a foreigner from another land.
But Boaz had seen Ruth's faithfulness.
Through life's trials she had stood the test.
So he answered, "The Lord is rewarding you;
under His wings you have found rest!"

With grace, Boaz offered both rest and
refreshing as Ruth submitted before him.
This is so like Christ, the Lord of the harvest,
offering rest from our burden of sin.   Matthew 11:28
Ruth requested of Boaz that both
Naomi's and her security be assured.
Boaz perceived Ruth's virtue, and
to her he gave his word.
He redeemed the land of Elimelech
for Naomi; Ruth became his wife,
as was the custom of that day.
Many witnessed that the Lord was building
"the house of Israel" in his own special way!

Ruth conceived, and to Boaz, a
son, Obed, she did bear.
And in her old age Naomi was rewarded,
for Obed was considered her heir!
As David's great-grandmother, Ruth
was an ancestor of the Messiah
though she came from the Moabite nation.
Through this story, we realize God's inclusive
love is for the faithful in all His creation.

***

A Godly woman named Hannah was   1 Samuel 1–8
barren; longing for a child, she prayed,
"I'll give him to you for your service, oh
Lord." This was the promise she made.
God heard Hannah's prayer, and Samuel
was born, but at a very young age, she
took him to the house of the Lord;
by Eli the priest he'd be raised.
One night, Samuel was awakened from
sleep; "Samuel, Samuel," a voice came.
Though at first confused, Samuel then
realized it was God who was calling his name!
"Speak, for your servant hears," he replied.
God's message was against Eli; the corruption
he had allowed could not be denied.
Should Samuel tell Eli when he asked?
This was something he'd have to decide.
Samuel revealed all that God told him;
God's message he could not hide.
That Samuel was God's chosen prophet
became known both far and wide.

Of all the judges of Israel,
Samuel was the very last.
Many times he cried out to the
Lord on his people's behalf.
When Israel feared their enemy and
lamented their sin, Samuel warned,
"Return to your God; serve only Him!
Put away foreign gods that are in your land; then
God will save you from the Philistines' hand!"

Samuel witnessed the time when God's
Holy Arc was captured by Philistine men.
But they soon experienced the power
of God, whose glory dwelt therein.
Plagued with tumors and destruction,
they were sorely vexed.
They returned the Arc to Israel,
fearing death would come next.

The Elders of Israel came to Samuel
with a special request,
"Give us a king instead of a judge; we
want to be like all of the rest." Samuel was
saddened; he prayed, and God answered,
"It is Me, not you, whom the people
reject; rebellion against My rule
is what their words reflect!
Heed the voice of the people and give
them a king; but forewarn them of the
changes that a kingdom will bring.

Saul, from the tribe of Benjamin,   1 Samuel 9–15
was anointed Israel's first king.
He followed not the commands of
God; instead he did his own thing.
King Saul would need to be replaced; with
his disobedience, he had brought disgrace.

God said, "Samuel, fill your horn with   1 Samuel
oil to anoint the new king-to-be.   16–17
Go to the home of Jesse; several sons has he.
It's David, the shepherd boy, who
will replace King Saul.
It is he, the youngest son, on
whom My Spirit will fall."

As David had watched over his sheep using only
a rock and a sling, he was being prepared by God
to do an even greater thing!
He'd kill the Philistine giant, Goliath, who was
over nine feet tall.
A stone would strike Goliath in the forehead,
causing the giant to fall!
God would use this young shepherd who could
play the harp and sing to calm the spirit of Saul
until he himself became king.

***

Through King David, God's covenant was
extended; forever his throne would stand.   2 Samuel 7
The Davidic line, leading to Christ,
would be held in God's own hand.
With David as king, the tribes were united; his
godly leadership brought honor and glory.
He became a war hero, a poet of praise,
but that's not the end of the story!
The destroyer of all that is good is sin,   2 Samuel
and tragically, David's heart   11–12
allowed evil to enter in.
David's sin was with Bathsheba,
who was Uriah's wife.

After failing to conceal Bathsheba's
pregnancy, David took Uriah's life!
For a year, David lived in hypocrisy,
ignoring his guilt within.
But God sent Nathan, His prophet,
to confront him of his sin.
David's reaction was one of remorse;
true repentance and worship ensued.
But tragically sin had begun its course; through
the next generation its evil it spewed!
David prayed that God's mercy
might be extended to him,   Psalm 51
that God would blot out his
transgressions and sin.
"Create in me a clean heart, O God;
renew a right spirit within.
Restore to me salvation's joy; let my
lips speak forth your praises again."

Today, sin still crouches at our door,
just waiting to be let in.   *Genesis 4:7*
But we, as followers of Jesus Christ,   *Ephesians*
have His Spirit secured within.   *1:13–14*
Clothed with God's mighty armor, we
have His power as our sure defense.
The darkness that seeks to overpower us,
we have strength to stand against!

With salvation as our helmet and our   *Ephesians*
breastplate of His righteousness,   *6:10–18*
surrounded by truth, faith is our shield;
Our sword—His Word, we can wield
against the voices that call us to yield!
With a prayer on our lips and gospel sandals on
our feet, we are prepared, our armor complete!

***

In Jerusalem, on the mountain called Moriah,   1 Chronicles
David planned to build a house for his Lord.   22
Although he made abundant preparations,
God forbade him, saying, "You're
a man of the sword.
With Solomon, your son, the wars will cease;
I'll establish his throne and give him peace.
It is he who will build a house for My name;   2 Chronicles
Riches and wisdom will be his fame."   2:5–6

So Solomon built a temple, much
greater than any temple had been.
For Solomon stated, "Our God is greater;
even heaven cannot contain Him!"

God's greatness is beyond all measure—
much more than I can comprehend!
Through the face of His Son, Jesus,   *2 Corinthians*
the knowledge of His glory He does extend.   *4:6*

His promise is to remove our stony hearts;   *Ezekiel*
a new spirit within us He'll place.   *11:19–20*
He'll be our God, and we'll be His
Oh, the magnitude of His glorious grace!

King Solomon rose to great heights.   1 Kings 3–11
His power and achievements became legend!
But as is common to man, he
was not without flaw.
Carried away by success, he turned
aside from God's law.

God appeared before Solomon twice,
granting wisdom and extending His covenant.
When Solomon failed God and
his heart proved untrue,
God said, "I'll tear the kingdom from you!
But for the sake of David, my servant,
I'll not act till your reign is through.
The kingdom will be torn asunder as Rehoboam
begins his reign; but for David and Jerusalem's
sake, the tribe of Judah with him will remain."

A leader often determines the fate of his nation.
Sin doesn't just quietly rest!
Solomon's disobedience brought his nation to
failure, when instead, it could have been blessed.

Solomon's reign ended; his son   1 Kings 12
Rehoboam became king.
Under him there was a great revolution;
between Rehoboam and
Jeroboam, hostility grew.
With God still in control, the
kingdom split in two.

***

A succession of kings followed in both Israel and
Judah; with few exceptions, most defied God.
The final result of this downward trend?
Both North and South Kingdoms
would eventually end!

***

It was during this time in the Northern Kingdom   Jonah 1–4
that Jonah, God's servant, received his call.
God said, "Go to Nineveh, that city headed
straight for destruction; you'll be the messenger
I send to bring them My instruction.
Warn them that I, the Lord God
Almighty, am aware of their evil ways.
Without the repentance of their sin,
disaster will fall in forty days!"

Jonah rejected God's call to him; he boarded
a ship headed in the opposite direction.
For the Gentile people in Nineveh,
he shared not God's affection!
One cannot run away from God,
which Jonah soon discovered.
A great storm arose; he was tossed overboard;
there was no chance he'd be recovered!

But God, in His providence, had prepared a
huge fish, who swallowed Jonah that day!
In this helpless position, caused by
his own disposition, for three days
and three nights he did stay!
Jonah recognized his sin and the situation he
was in, and he called to his God for mercy.
Then by supernatural means, God intervened;
the great fish coughed up Jonah on shore!
The word of God was spoken to Jonah, "Go to
Nineveh with the message I gave you before!"

Reluctantly Jonah went to Nineveh and
did as he had been told. Although he still
lacked the compassion he needed,
His message to Nineveh was seriously heeded!
God saw their sorrow, and He had compassion
as they turned from their evil ways.
He relented the disaster that was to come
upon them, and gave them many more days.

God saw Jonah's attitude and
the anger he did display.
In His kindness He corrected him
in a very practical way.
His message to Jonah:
Nineveh's 120,000 people were
souls that God did cherish.
God had pity on them, not wishing
that any one of them should perish!   2 Peter 3: 9

During the reign of the kings, God's people were
not abandoned. Though provoked by their sin,
God sent prophets to them to remind
them what God had commanded.
"Humble yourselves; turn from
your sin and wicked ways.
Then God will hear you, cleanse and forgive
you, and return you to prosperous days."

***

Elijah was a prophet sent by God to the North.　　1 Kings 16–18
He proclaimed Jehovah God as
he boldly spoke forth.
King Ahab had set up an altar for
Baal, the god of his wife, Jezebel.
Elijah asked for a show of the true God's
power, and the fire of the Lord fell!

Other miracles were performed by Elijah as
the Spirit of the Lord gave him power:
He called rain to stop and begin
again only at a designated hour.
He multiplied food during the famine
and raised to life the widow's son.
He divided the Jordan's water and crossed
over when his work on earth was done.　　2 Kings
A horse-drawn chariot descended; in
a whirlwind Elijah was taken.
His mantle fell to Elisha, who with
the Spirit of God was shaken.

As the leadership of Israel changed from king to
king, no hint of repentance did anyone bring.
Each followed in the footsteps of their
fathers before, distancing themselves
from their God more and more!

Even as Elisha boldly confronted their evil and
confirmed Jehovah's power, they continued in
their sin, racing towards God's judgment hour!
Elisha's message for Israel continued for years;
but the words of the prophet fell on deaf ears.
The people "stiffened their necks,"
chose to live their own way.
They refused God's warnings,
rejecting what He had to say.

The Lord was very angry; He'd remove
them from His sight! Deliverance into
plunderer's hands was to be their awful
plight! Besieged by Assyria's mighty hand,
Israel was defeated, conquered, and
dispersed throughout the land!

***

Because of the spiritual and moral decadence
of Judah, their kingdom, too, was faltering.
The Southern Kingdom's sinful ways
would definitely need altering!
God had made a covenant with David
that His kingdom would remain.
But would Judah remember this promise,
repent, and from all evil restrain?
As usual, God was working His sovereign plan;
and as usual, He chose to work through a man.

Isaiah witnessed a call as God's holiness   Isaiah 6–9
was portrayed in a vision.
This led Isaiah to a humble confession,
cleansing, and a commission!
Speaking for God, Isaiah's message was
one of both mercy and judgment:
"Though your sins be as scarlet,
they shall be as white as snow;
though they be red as crimson,
they shall be as wool.   Isaiah 1:18–20
If you are willing to obey, you'll
be forgiven by the Lord;
But if you refuse and rebel, you'll
be devoured by the sword!"

Speaking for God, Isaiah foretold how
God's ultimate plan would unfold:
Through a remnant of His chosen people
the Davidic promise would be fulfilled.
"For unto us a child is born,
unto us a son is given."
In the future a virgin would give birth—
Messiah would come, ushering
God's kingdom to earth!
Despised and rejected by man, He would be   Isaiah 52–53
As a lamb to the slaughter,
He'd be led to the tree!
*Freely offering His life for man's
sin and insurrection,
He'd face separation from His
Father before resurrection.*

Speaking for God, Isaiah also foretold
of the future return of Messiah we've
yet to behold: "Wonderful, Counselor,
Mighty God, Everlasting, Father, and
Prince of Peace is His name."
With righteousness and justice,
in peace He will reign!
For time and eternity His
government will remain!

Speaking for God, Isaiah shared his   Isaiah 65–66
visions of a glorious new creation.
At the end of time, the heavens and earth
will undergo a complete transformation!
In the new heavens and earth, voices
of weeping will not be heard.
The wolf will become the lamb's friend.
God will rejoice and find joy in His people.
True worship and peace will not end!

***

God appointed other great prophets to   Hebrews 11
speak forth His word. Major and minor
prophets made their voices heard.
Many suffered persecution;
some died by the sword.
But their faithfulness was evident
as they stood for their Lord!

***

Jeremiah was one of the great prophets of
old; a prophet from birth called to be.
Judah's future destruction because of
their sin, God allowed him to foresee.
Known as the "weeping prophet," Jeremiah
foretold Judah of their coming doom.
His life was one of ridicule, imprisonment,
persecution, and gloom.
But he kept to the task, not wanting to
fail, condemning false prophets who
cried, "Peace! Peace!" to no avail.

Jeremiah

***

The heart of God was breaking under
the load of man's awful sin.
God, abhorring evil, must pronounce
judgment; righteousness would win!
Through Ezekiel, both prophet and priest,
God's purpose for judgment was stated:
"Then they will know I AM the Lord their
God." Against Me all sin originated.

Ezekiel

Ezekiel also disclosed God's love and concern
for the remnant of believers who would return.
Israel would undergo restoration; the
temple rebuilt; the people, one nation.
God's promise to them would ever be true;

Ezekiel 11

"I'll give them one heart; their spirit I'll renew.
I'll replace their stony heart with
a heart made of flesh,
So they'll walk in My ways;
their sins they'll confess.
They will be My people, and their God I will be.
We'll be united once more—a people set free!"

***

Josiah was one of Judah's God-fearing kings.   2 Kings 22–23
A temporary return to God his story brings:
He sought the God of his father, David,
and destroyed the idols and shrines.
While repairing the temple, the book
of the Law of the Lord, he finds.
When God's Law was read to Josiah,
he tore his clothes in great sorrow;
He'd follow the Lord this very day
and also for all his tomorrows.
God honored his humility and tenderness
of heart, and kept him from witnessing
the calamity soon to start.

In spite of Josiah and a few others like him,
the Kingdom of Judah returned to their sin!
The wrath of God rose; there was no remedy.
Conquered by the Babylonians,
Judah suffered captivity!

***

After King Nebuchadnezzar's Jewish conquest,   Daniel 1–6
he chose young Hebrew youths—
the brightest and best.
As they served in his court, he'd change
their names and teach them his ways.
Little did he know God was with
them, guiding their days.

Daniel and his three friends were
among those who were selected.
The king would soon realize they
were not what he had expected!
Orders were given that to Daniel
were wrong; his faith and prayer life
with his God kept him strong.

King Nebuchadnezzar experienced a dream,
the meaning of which he could not understand.
"Tell me my dream and its interpretation," of
his wise men and astrologers he did demand.
None of these men could do what he asked,
For without God's help, this
was an impossible task!
Furiously, the king ordered
them to face execution.
But Daniel trusted God for a solution.

He requested the king give him time before
telling him the dream and its interpretation.
He and his companions faithfully sought
their God in great anticipation.
God, in His mercy, revealed the dream
to Daniel in a vision in the night.
Daniel blessed the name of his God
forever for all His wisdom and might.

Giving God all the glory, Daniel revealed
the dream and what it foretold:
Babylon was the kingdom represented
by the image's head made of gold.
It would be the first of four great Gentile powers.
In time three more kingdoms would
rule for their God-given hours.
The final kingdom will be one God
designs; it will be His rule and reign.
All other kingdoms will be consumed, but
forever His will remain! The king rewarded
Daniel for his revelation, promoting
him to chief of his administration.
Nebuchadnezzar recognized
Daniel's God to be the God of
gods, but little did he know
That in his knowledge of the Almighty
God, he had a ways to go!

In pride, King Nebuchadnezzar constructed
a ninety-foot image of gold.
When music was sounded, all people
were expected to do as they were told.
"Fall down and worship the image I've
made, and no harm will come to you;
But fail to obey, and it will be your last
day as a fiery furnace awaits you."

To three Hebrew men—Shadrach, Meshach, and
Abed-Nego—this posed a great test of their faith.
But they refused the decree that said,
"Bow your knee" to any God
except Jehovah, their own!

Bound and taken to the furnace, the
three men into the fire were cast.
The king was there watching, as he knew
their deaths would be exceedingly fast!
But in astonishment he proclaimed,
"I see four men walking in the fire unchained!"
The men were called out of the furnace; on
their bodies the fire had had no power!
The Most High God had been with them,
even joining them during their trial hour!

The genuineness of our faith,
which is more precious than perishable gold,
will be refined by fire, making us more
like our Savior when Him we behold!   *1 Peter 1:7*

***

Daniel and his friends were promoted
to high places in Babylon
Little did Nebuchadnezzar realize
his reign was nearly done.
God used Daniel and a dream to
bring Nebuchadnezzar to reason that
it was the Sovereign God who allowed
him to rule for his given season.

The king was told he'd be driven from his
throne and dwell as a beast of the field.
The lesson? Heaven rules and to the
Most High God you must yield!
Yet in pride, Nebuchadnezzar still declared
Babylon the product of his own glory and power.
A voice from heaven sounded; the
dream was fulfilled that very hour!

His insanity led him to the field;
as an animal he'd graze.
But as he lifted his eyes toward
heaven, his understanding returned,
and he gave God praise—
"The Most High God rules the kingdom of men;
Its leaders He will decide.
His works are truth and His ways are just;
He brings those down who walk in pride."
When his trial ended, and the
kingdom was restored,
Nebuchadnezzar realized God
was the Almighty Lord!

Babylon was a magnificent city. Its
fame had spread far and wide.
Because of its mighty fortress,
all people felt safe inside.
Its walls were 350 feet tall with
200 lookout towers;
"Surely we are impenetrable against
all the outside powers!"

***

The next king of Babylon was Belshazzar,
known for his wild parties.
Though his city was being besieged
by the Persians and the Medes, he
summoned his lords to a feast.

They praised their gods of gold, silver, iron,
bronze, wood, and stone, as they drank from the
holy vessels meant for the worship of God alone!
At that very blasphemous moment the
fingers of a giant hand did appear!
They wrote words of warning on the
wall as everyone stood in fear.
Terror struck Belshazzar and sent him into
shock; so much so that his knees began to knock!

"Find me a man who understands these words,
and I'll reward him with prestige and power!"
But none was found in the entire land, who
could explain the words written by the hand.
That is, not until they remembered Daniel,
in whom God's Spirit did dwell.
So the interpretation of God's message,
on the prophet Daniel fell:
Belshazzar's days had been numbered; he'd been
weighed in the balances and found wanting!
The Medes and Persians would
conquer his kingdom!
The message was certainly haunting!

That very night, Belshazzar was slain, and
Darius, the Mede, began his reign.
Babylon, the kingdom represented
by the head of gold, had now fallen
to the second Gentile kingdom, as
Nebuchadnezzar's first dream had told.

***

OMWG OH, MY WONDERFUL GOD!

Among all the leaders Darius chose,
Daniel was his favored one.
Daniel's excellent spirit and faultless ways did
not go unnoticed but earned him praise.

Cunningly, Daniel's jealous peers contrived
a plan to defeat him: they drafted a law
they knew Daniel could not and would
not obey; it stated, "To no one but the
king can anyone petition or pray."
The punishment for disobedience was
both hard and fast—into a hungry lions'
den, the person would be cast!

Daniel heard that the king had signed
the decree, but in devotion to his
God, he still bowed his knee.
He loved his Lord more than his
very own life, and knew God to be
faithful amid harmony or strife.

When informed of Daniel, Darius regretted
the day that he signed that awful decree.
Now Daniel, whom he admired, must
face the lions; by law, it had to be!
That night, he fasted on Daniel's behalf,
knowing Daniel's God was great.
He rose early the next morn and went
in haste straight to the lions' gate.

"Daniel," he called. "Have you been saved
by the God to whom you belong?"
Daniel replied, "My God sent His angel
so mighty and strong, to close the lions'
mouths because I've done no wrong!"

Darius ordered that Daniel be freed;
and shortly thereafter, he decreed,
"All subjects of mine must honor
the God that Daniel serves;
He is the living God and His
kingdom forever endures!"

Daniel is an example of a life lived
with purpose, power, and prayer.
It carries a special challenge: Be
a Daniel if you dare!
But that's not the complete story of
God's mission for this man;
For God had even more for Daniel in His plan.

Six revelatory visions God allowed Daniel to see;   Daniel 7–12
the messages of the visions disclosed
what would come to be.
In one of his visions, Daniel saw coming
on a cloud, one like the Son of Man.
He was presented with glory, kingship, and
dominion over all people of every land.

When Jesus called Himself the Son of Man, Jewish
leaders understood who He claimed to be.
For they had been instructed by the prophet
Daniel but failed to believe this was He!   *Matthew 11:19*

All of Daniel's other visions are prophetic
messages to instruct and to give us stability,
knowing that whatever happens, all of God's
ransomed children will rise triumphantly!

***

God had not forgotten His people,
so long in exile held.   Jeremiah
Soon they would be brought back to the   25:11–12
land in which they once had dwelled.   Isaiah 44:28
One hundred years before Cyrus was born,
his life by God had been anointed.   Isaiah 45:1–7
To allow the return of the Jews to Judah
was the task he was appointed.

Cyrus was now king of Persia with the   Ezra 1–6
Hebrews under his command;
God moved the heart of Cyrus
to help him understand.
Cyrus honored God's sovereignty over him
as to the Hebrews he spoke these words:
"Go back to Jerusalem and rebuild
the temple to your Lord.
I'll give back the temple treasures, which
all these years have been stored."

God also moved the hearts of His people
as they heard this proclamation.
They knew their God was speaking to them—
the holy city of Jerusalem was their destination!

Over forty thousand exiles departed with
gifts of gold, silver, livestock, and more,
each returning to the Judean town
where he had lived before.
Led to Jerusalem by Jeshua and Zerubbabel,
they rebuilt the altar, and sacrifices were
made; Priests and Levites praised the Lord
as the foundation of God's house was laid.

Enemies of the Israelites brought threats, causing
the construction of the temple to cease.
But God was there through His
prophets, Haggai and Zechariah,
offering his strength and peace.
By a decree of King Darius, the temple
was completed and dedicated—each
worker celebrated with joy in his heart.
For they knew that their Lord was there, working
for them, as the Gentile kings played their part.

Though they honored their God   Ezra 7–10
with sacrifice and celebration,
God still had further plans for
their spiritual reformation.
God would use Ezra, a faithful scribe and
priest, to reinstate the Law of the Lord.
For there were still statutes God had given
that were presently being ignored.

The hand of God was on Ezra, as
King Artaxerxes gave his consent
for Ezra and company to travel and
join the Jerusalem remnant.
Ezra's call to repentance and renewal of faith
brought the Israelites to true confession.
Their hearts were broken before their God
at the gravity of their transgression.
After confessing their guilt, as they saw the light,
they sought to make changes to set things right.

This is how it is even today—to remain
in sin is not God's way. But our God
is faithful, righteous, and just.
He remembers our frame—that we are but dust.   Psalm 103:14
Our humility is necessary; confession a must.
He'll forgive us our sins if in Him we trust.   1 John 1:9
What God desires is a heart that is changed
Just ask, seek, and knock to see life rearranged!   Matthew 7:7

***

Many Jews remained in Persia, not   Esther 1–8
returning to Judah, their homeland.
But divine providence ruled over human
affairs to save them from the enemy's hand.
Mordecai and his cousin Esther lived
in Susa during this very hour;
King Ahasuerus, who had just banished his
queen, was the monarch presently in power.

A search was made for girls of great beauty,
who would have a chance to become queen.
Esther, who was chosen among many,
kept her Jewish identity hidden; for
her to become queen with her heritage,
would surely have been forbidden.

Mordecai had been a parent to Esther, as she
had been orphaned at a very young age.
Now he was given by the providence of
God an extra portion of courage.

Haman, a descendant of a nation with
a long-lasting hatred of Jews,
had just been promoted to a high position—
this was definitely not good news!
He demanded that all honor him and
before him they bow their knee.
When Mordecai refused to do so,
Haman considered him a rebel to be!
He accused all Jews of being a potential threat;
his edict to purge his country of them,
with the king's approval, was met!

Exodus
17:6–18

When he learned of all that Haman had planned,
Mordecai tore his clothes in great sorrow.
Now, only Esther, in the royal court,
could bring a safe tomorrow.

A copy of the edict with Haman's
unspeakable plans, to Queen Esther
was relayed, urging her to appeal to the
king; her action must not be delayed!
"Dear Esther, speak with King Ahasuerus,
from annihilation you must save us!
It is imperative for all of our lives that
you make an attempt, for when it is
discovered you are Jewish. even you,
oh Queen, will not be exempt!"

After three days of fasting, Esther approached
the king on behalf of the Jewish nation.
She asked for his mercy to allow the Jews
to defend themselves in this horrid situation.

Haman's plot was discovered;
Mordecai's good deeds uncovered; the
Jews destroyed their tormentors!
Esther proclaimed days of celebration;
divine providence had saved her nation!
This, Esther and Mordecai were meant for!

***

Nehemiah, a cupbearer in King
Artaxerxes's court,
received from Jerusalem a disturbing report.
Though the temple had been built, the
gates were burned with fire, and the walls
were broken down! Nothing kept their
enemies from infiltrating their town!

Nehemiah mourned and fasted as
he prayed for several days,
"Oh, Lord God of Heaven, I
confess our sinful ways!"
God put in his heart that to rebuild the wall
was what he was to do; his determination and
dependence on his God would see him through.
His request to go to Jerusalem was
granted by the Persian king.
Gifts of courage and administration
to Jerusalem he would bring.

Nehemiah

He rallied the people of God to the task;
help from his Lord he did not fail to ask!
Many times Nehemiah received enemies'
threats, schemes to discourage and harm.
But Nehemiah insisted his workers be ready
to fight; he gave the command to bear arms.
In spite of intense enemy opposition,
he inspired the people to press on.
He gave encouragement while praying for
strength—it was His God he relied upon.

The wall was completed in 52 days; all
assembled together to give God praise.
The people all stood at attention; the
Book of God's Law, Ezra read.
Then they fell down and wept as they were
instructed concerning what the law said.
But Nehemiah spoke, "This day is for
celebration! Do not mourn nor weep.
For the joy of the Lord is your strength as
the Feast of the Tabernacles you keep!"
True repentance followed; respect
for God's law was revived.
Watchmen, singers, and Levites were appointed
to their tasks as the law described. Through
Nehemiah, God's appointed man of the hour,
the Israelite nation was once more empowered.

God often called man to "stand in the   *Ezekiel 22:30*
gap" on behalf of His people
in a time of desperation.
Noah, Joseph, Moses, Esther, and Nehemiah were
His instruments during a critical situation.
God's final deliverer was Jesus Christ, who
gave Himself to usher in our salvation.

***

Through one final prophet God chose to speak;   Malachi 1–4
using questions and answers, Malachi
did seek to offer wise counsel to
those whose faith was faltering;
He reminded them their God was forever the
same; it was their attitudes that needed altering!
This is what the Lord Almighty says:
"Return to Me, and I will return to you;
I'll throw open the floodgates of heaven and pour
abundant blessings; test Me to see what I'll do!"

Those who feared the Lord gathered together
to talk, as the Lord God listened and heard.
A book of remembrance was written before Him
for those who honored His word.
He called them His treasured possession
among those who would receive His reward:
"The Sun of Righteousness will rise with healing
in His wings; the wicked will be trampled
as His righteous judgment He brings!"   Malachi 4:2–3

Those who had faith in this future
Messianic promise were counted as
righteous, their salvation secured.   *Ephesians 2:8*
Just as we today are counted as righteous
by our faith in Christ, God's Word.   *John 1:1*

God delivered His final message
through His servant Malachi.
Then in His sovereignty, He paused and
allowed over four hundred years to go by!
The ways of God are beyond our grasp;   *Isaiah 55:9*
His timing is not our time.
It seems man has to exhaust self-effort to
receive the intervention of the Divine

***

As Greek and then Roman powers
dominated the world,
Israel searched for her place to belong.
Several factions arose, each seeking answers;
but all human efforts seemed to go wrong!

It was into this world of very great need that
God announced the coming of His Son.   *John 3:16*
The greatest love story was unfolding;
the Christian era had now begun!

The promised Messiah, God incarnate would be;
fully human, yet fully divine was He!
Conceived by the Spirit, yet
through woman he came.
From the moment of His birth, the
world was never the same!

***

An angel was sent to the priest Zechariah   Luke 1
with a message he could scarcely believe.
Although his wife, Elizabeth, was
advanced in years, a special child,
her first, she would conceive.

He'd be born just a short time
before the Messiah; preparing the
way, he'd ask man to repent.
In the spirit and power of Elijah,
John the Baptist by God would be sent.

To the virgin Mary of Nazareth,
the angel Gabriel did appear:
"Rejoice, highly favored one;
the Lord is with you!"
Mary's first reaction was surprise mixed with fear!
But the angel continued,
"Do not be afraid, for you have
found favor with God.
By the Holy Spirit you will conceive
and bring forth a son.
Call His name Jesus. He will be great—
for He is God's Anointed One!"

Mary believed that with God
all things were possible.
She would be the maidservant of her Lord.
Although she had little knowledge of
the future, she answered, "Let it be
to me according to your word!"
Mary's destiny was confirmed with a visit to
Elizabeth, who was also pregnant with a boy.
For when Mary entered her
house and gave greeting,
Elizabeth exclaimed, "The babe in
my womb just leaped for joy!"

There must have been great conversation as
these two women rejoiced together as one.
For God, in all His sovereignty, had chosen to use
them in preparation for the coming of His Son!

***

Joseph also received an angelic message;   Matthew 1
it came to him in a dream:
"Joseph, son of David, take Mary
your betrothed to be your wife.
The prophecy concerning the coming
Messiah is being fulfilled through her life."
Joseph believed the angel's announcement
and did as he was commanded.
An earthly father to the Son of God?—a
future far greater than he had planned it!

Following these supernatural visits and the
revelation that they'd been chosen by God,
I've often wondered how Mary and Joseph felt,
as reality returned their feet to earth's sod!

OMWG OH, MY WONDERFUL GOD!

I surmise that their faith increased more and more,
as they experienced Isaiah's promise
given hundreds of years before:

Their strength was renewed as   Isaiah 40:31
they waited on the Lord;
through all doubts and confusion,
on eagle's wings they soared!
They ran and were not weary; they
walked and did not faint; because they
lifted their eyes toward heaven,
realizing their Lord knew their every complaint!

So for us today, why do we doubt?
Why is our faith so small?
Why do we question our God when
He has power over all!
His Word says,   Philippians
"Be anxious for nothing; in thanksgiving   4:6–7
make your requests known.
His peace through Christ that passes all
understanding can become our very own!"

"Go to the city of your origin;   Luke 2
a census must be taken."
This was the decree sent out by
Caesar Augustus of Rome.
So Joseph and Mary traveled to Bethlehem,
leaving their Nazareth home.

It must have been a hard journey for
Mary, who was to give birth very soon.
Upon arrival, they spent the night in a
stable; it was the only available room!

It was there on that night that Mary gave birth;
Jesus, "the Lord who saves,"
had come to this earth!
Jesus was wrapped in swaddling clothes
and laid in a manger filled with hay.
Coming to earth in this humble
manner was God Himself.
Oh, what a glorious day!!

The incarnation of God illustrated
His love for all mankind.   *John 3:16*
Gentiles, as well as His chosen Jews,
were always on His mind.   *Genesis 12:3*
Mentioned in Christ's genealogy is Rahab,
the harlot, who hid Joshua's spies.   *Isaiah 42:6*
She was the mother of Boaz whom Ruth the
Moabite marries after her husband dies.
Ruth was Jesse's grandmother,
and David was Jesse's son.
Through the lineage of David, the Christ was
born, but God's plan was for everyone!

On Bethlehem's hillside, shepherds were caring   Luke 2
for their sheep on that advent night. Suddenly,
the sky erupted with the brightest blinding light!
"Do not be afraid," spoke an angel,
"For all, I bring news of great joy!
In the city of David, a Savior has been born.
In a manger you'll find this boy!
Glory to God in the Highest!
Peace and good will to men on earth!"
The heavenly host filled the sky with their
praises proclaiming the Messiah's birth!

As the angels returned to the heavens,
the shepherds hastened on their way.
To see the Christ Child with their very own eyes
would be their most memorable day!
How special they must have felt that night,
being the first to receive the word!
They returned rejoicing and praising
God for all they had seen and heard!

Two devout Jews, Simeon and Anna, had
waited for years in great expectation,
longing to see—before their death—the
Child of God's promised Salvation.
Now when Jesus was brought to the temple to be
presented to the Lord, they blessed the child and
praised their God for the fulfillment of His word.

As Simeon held the child, his prayer to
God was a prophecy for all who heard.
That this child was destined for an eternal
purpose was evident in every word!
"Now, Oh Lord, release me to your promised
peace, for my eyes have seen your Salvation—
This is the promise that You have prepared
for the people of every nation.
To Israel, He's their glory, their
great Consolation.
To the Gentiles, He's the Light
to bring revelation.

This Child is chosen by God to reveal
the innermost hearts of all.   Isaiah 8:14–15
Acceptance or rejection of Him will
cause either their rise or fall.
As the thoughts of many hearts are disclosed,
Mary, even your own soul to a
sword will be exposed!"   John 19:25

**

Wise Men from the East had   Matthew 2
been traveling from afar,
seeking the Child whose birth was
announced by the appearance of a star.
Reaching Jerusalem, the wise men
inquired, "Where is He who has
been born King of the Jews?"
To wicked King Herod, the possibility
of another king was horrifying news!
*Herod had already committed several
murders in order to save his throne.
Now he would seek information concerning
this birth—he must remain king all alone!*

The Wise Men were sent on to Bethlehem.
With the star guiding them, their way was sure.
Rejoicing when they found Jesus, they
fell down to worship, offering gifts of
gold, frankincense, and myrrh.
They were warned in a dream not to
return to Jerusalem. Herod's interest
in King Jesus was a disguise!
For Herod meant to harm the Child;
His words had all been lies!

**

When the Wise Men departed, an angel
appeared to Joseph in a dream:
"Arise! Take Mary and the young boy,
for Herod is seeking Him to destroy!
Go to Egypt, and stay there
until I bring you word.
In Egypt your safety will be assured!"
So Joseph arose and took Jesus and his
mother in the darkness of the night.
Hosea's prophecy was being fulfilled
as to Egypt they took their flight!   Hosea 11:1

After King Herod died, an angel again
appeared to Joseph and said,
"Go to Israel, for it is safe since the
child's enemies are now dead."
So Joseph, Mary, and Jesus returned
and were guided to Galilee.
The city of Nazareth was the place
where Jesus was meant to be.

***

The grace of God rested on Jesus as   Luke 2
He grew, became strong in spirit,
and was filled with wisdom beyond His years.
His conversation at the temple during
Passover astonished the Jewish scholars;
they couldn't believe their ears!
They were amazed at the knowledge, questions,
and answers of this young twelve-year-old!
Upon discovering Jesus was still in the
temple, His parents began to scold:
"Son, your father and I have been
anxiously searching for You!"
His answer: "Didn't you know My
Father's business is what I must do?"

Mary remembered all she had
learned about Jesus,
although she didn't fully understand.
Jesus increased in both wisdom and stature,
and found favor with God and man.

***

The word of God came to John the Baptist;   John 1
in the power of the Spirit he preached.
Multitudes listened, questioned, and responded,
as the whole region of the Jordan he reached.

He preached about the presence of sin
and their great need to confess.
"Repent, for the Kingdom of Heaven is at
hand," spoke the voice from the wilderness.

In expectation, some thought
John to be the Christ,
which John was quick to deny!
"I baptize with water, but One mightier
than I will baptize with the Spirit—His
sandal, I'm not worthy to untie!"

When John saw Jesus coming toward him,
the Holy Spirit prompted him to say,
"Behold the Lamb of God,
who takes our sin away!
I need to be baptized by You,
and yet you come to me?"
Jesus answered, "To fulfill all
righteousness, this is meant to be!"

As Jesus came up from the water, the heavens
opened above, and the Spirit of God descended
upon Him in the form of a beautiful dove.
Suddenly, a voice from the heavens sounded,
"This is my Beloved Son, in whom I delight!"
John was a witness of the Holy Trinity
of God! What a glorious sight!

After His baptism, Jesus was led by   Matthew 4
the Spirit to the wilderness.
It was there He would meet the devil,
who would put Him to the test.
Jesus fasted for forty days and nights,
and Satan saw His need:
"Here, turn these stones into bread;
from Your hunger you'll be freed!"

"Man shall not live by bread alone!"
Jesus used God's words to reply.
To the physical life bread might bring
satisfaction, but man's spirit still would die.

The devil then took Jesus to Jerusalem; on
the pinnacle of the temple He sat above all!
"If you truly are the Son of God, throw
Yourself down, for He will command
His angels to save you from the fall!"

Again, Jesus resisted Satan; the
sword of the Spirit, He thrust!
"It is written, you shall not tempt
the Lord your God!"
In His Father's word He placed His trust!

Then Satan took Jesus to an exceedingly
high mountain to show Him the
world's kingdoms and their glory.
"All this can be Yours if You worship me!"
(A shortcut to a kingdom without the cross-story!)

"Get behind Me, Satan!" *(Jesus had nerve!)*
"It is written, worship the Lord your
God. Him only shall you serve!"
Through all the temptations Jesus followed
God's will—He did not succumb to sin!
As Satan retreated, the angels
came to minister onto Him.

***

Jesus first miracle was at a wedding where   John 2
they failed to have enough wine.
Mary, His mother, came to Jesus
asking for a miraculous sign.
She instructed the servants, "Whatever
Jesus says, be sure that you do."
Having no idea what was to happen,
they still would follow through.
Jesus instructed, "Take the six water pots
and fill them with water up to the brim.
Then draw a cup from the pot, find the master
of the feast, and give the cup to him."
As he drank from the cup, the master
exclaimed, "Usually the better wine
is first served to the guests,
But this wine I am drinking
is definitely the best!"
Jesus's disciples witnessed the miracle
of the water turned to wine, as
He manifested His glory.
Proving His Deity in His power to create
is just another part of Jesus's story.

Jesus began His ministry by proclaiming to be   Luke 4
the fulfillment of Old Testament prophesy.
In His hometown of Nazareth
on a certain Sabbath Day,
Jesus was in a synagogue reading from the
scroll of Isaiah; this is what He had to say:
"'The Spirit of the Lord is upon me.
He has anointed Me to bring
the gospel to the poor,
to heal the brokenhearted and
sight to the blind, restore.
To proclaim pardon for the captives
and give them liberty, to set free the
oppressed—those crushed by tragedy.
This is the time of God's favor, when
the kingdom presents its Savior!'"

When He finished, the crowd waited   Isaiah 61:1–2
for His teaching on what they had just
heard. Responding to their expectation,
He spoke to them this word:
"The person to whom the prophet was
referring is standing before you today."
In disbelief, the listeners reacted,
"Isn't this Joseph's son?"
In anger, they pursued Him, but He walked
through the crowd and went on His way.

Rejected by His own country, Jesus
traveled to Capernaum in Galilee.
He healed the sick and cast out evil
spirits, as He spoke with authority.
The crowds followed Jesus as He walked
down by the sea to continue on His
way; they desired to see more and
hear more of what He had to say.

***

Of those who had followed Jesus to hear   Matthew 4, 10
His teachings and His miracles to see,
Jesus called twelve disciples and
gave them authority.
He instructed them to preach that the Kingdom
of Heaven was at hand and that evil spirits
and disease would flee at their command.
Of those He called, there were four
fishermen, two sets of brothers—
Simon, called Peter, and Andrew were first,
then James and John were the others.
There was James, the son of Alphaeus,
Philip and Bartholomew,
Thomas, Simon, Thaddaeus, and Matthew too.
He called Judas Iscariot, who a
traitor would become.
These were the men who walked and talked
with Jesus until His work on earth was done!

Jesus continued His ministry identifying God
as His Father and Himself as God's only Son.
(To the Pharisees and teachers of the
law, this was blasphemy 101!)
They questioned His power to forgive
and His activity on the Sabbath Day.
His association with "sinners" caused them
to grumble. They sought to put Him away!

Jesus retreated to a mountainside   Matthew 5–7
to teach His disciples
about pride and those who knew
evil came from within:
"Blessed are those who are humble in spirit,
meek, and mourn concerning their sin.
Blessed are those who hunger for righteousness;
for they will be satisfied. Blessed are the merciful;
to them God's mercy will not be denied!
Blessed are the pure in heart; for their
God they will definitely see!
Blessed are those who make peace in
their lives; the children of God they will
be! Blessed are those who are persecuted
because of their association with Me!
Along with the prophets before
them, great their reward will be!
You, My disciples, are the salt of the earth
and the light to a world in need.
Let your light shine so men will give praise
to the Father for your every good deed."

"Do not think I came to destroy the Law.
I did not come to destroy it but fulfill!"
Jesus is the only Man who kept the whole law
of God from the moment of His birth;
His is the only righteousness worthy of the Kingdom
of Heaven; and He gives it to all believers on earth.   Romans 10:4

Jesus was the "Word of God who
became flesh and dwelt among us."   John 1:14
To no other authority was it
necessary for him to appeal.
As He explained each moral commandment,
its full truth He did reveal.
"You have heard it said…But I say unto you…"
The crowds of people were astonished
when Jesus's teaching of the
commandments was through.

He continued,
"Do not worry; instead ask, seek, and
knock—God will take care of you.
Do not judge or behave hypocritically, for
God knows your motives in all that you do.
Beware of false prophets; discern
those who are true.
Do unto to others as you would
have them do unto you.

There's only one Master whom you
should serve; don't allow money to replace
God—your worship He deserves.
Let your charity to others, your prayers
and fasting be between God and you.
Don't try to get attention and
honor as the hypocrites do.
Lay up treasures in heaven and
not on earth below.
Take the narrow road that leads to life;
on the wide road many will go."

*No one had ever heard such wisdom as
expressed from the lips of this Man.
Could He really, truly be the Great I AM?*

***

Jesus also gave an example of
how we should pray:
"Father in Heaven, we honor
Your holy name this day.
May Your Kingdom to our earth come.
As in heaven, may Your will
on this earth be done.
Give us this day the food that we need.
Forgive us of each sinful thought or deed.
Help us forgive others the wrong they have done.
Rescue us from the evil one.
Forever and ever Your kingdom will reign,
with power and glory—forever the same."

***

The unbelief of the Jewish leaders only   John 8
increased with Jesus's teaching.
"You will die in your sins because
you won't believe I am He.
But if you abide in my word,
the truth will set you free!
Before Abraham was, I AM! You
don't believe what I say.
You are not like your ancestor Abraham
who rejoiced to see My day!"

In His ministry Jesus also proclaimed,
"All power in heaven and on earth
God has given to me."
When His disciples were in a boat, a mighty   Matthew
tempest arose, but Jesus calmed the troubled sea.   8: 23-27

Jesus had authority over creation, power over
the elements. *This should come as no surprise—*
for all things were created by Him and for
Him, including the land, the sea, and skies!

***

Both spiritual and physical life were
under Jesus' authority and command.
When Jesus was teaching, the crowds gathered
around Him; there was scarcely room to stand!
Some friends of a paralytic lowered him through
the roof—the only way they could get him in!
Jesus saw their faith and said, "Son,
I forgive you of your sin!"
The scribes observed and reasoned
in their hearts—why does this man
speak blasphemies like this?
Who can forgive sins but God alone?
Perceiving their thoughts, Jesus
said, "So you may know the Son of
Man has power to forgive sins,
'Paralytic, arise, take up your
bed and walk home'!"
Immediately he did so, and he
heard the amazed crowds say,
"We have witnessed remarkable things today!"   Mark 2:1–12

***

A Pharisee named Nicodemus came secretly   John 3
to Jesus in the middle of the night.
Jesus perceived the heart of this religious
man was seeking life-changing insight.
So Jesus told him, "You must be born again!
This is not a physical, but a spiritual
birth—one deep in the heart within."
Jesus went on to explain that
because of His great love,
God sent His Son to be the Savior of the world.
He Himself was that Son; through
Him, eternal life was unfurled!
He came to save, not condemn; the
Light had come; believe in Him!   John 4

Jesus identified Himself as the "Living
Water" to the woman at the well.
Amazed at all He revealed about her, she
left her water pot and went forth to tell.
"Come see this man! He could be the promised
Christ! Everything about me He knew!"
The Samaritans came to Jesus to see for
themselves if what this woman said was true.
After hearing all He had to say,
many more believed.
They recognized Jesus as the Christ;
the "Living Water" they received!

"Go home, for your son will live," Jesus said
to the nobleman whose son was dying.
He spoke words of healing to a lame man   John 5
who by Bethesda's Pool was lying.
Power to prolong life, power to restore!
Never had such divine power been
seen by these witnesses before!

The Jewish leaders sought to kill
Jesus—He healed on the Sabbath
and claimed an equal with God to be!
(If this was the messiah, certainly he'd
come as a warrior, set up a Jewish
government, and we would be set free!)
Jesus answered and spoke this to them:
"To honor the Father, if in Him you really
believed, then the authority He has given
to His Son, by you must be received!
For life and judgment are through the Son.
I seek not My own will, but that
the Father's be done!"

Jesus continued, "Four witnesses
I have that I am the Son:
There's John, who for a time was
a shining light to you,
and My works that the Father
has given Me to do.
My Father Himself testified of Me.
The scriptures speak the truth
that will set you free!
But You are not willing to
believe and come to Me.
Moses's law on which your hopes
are set, will your accuser be!"

Jesus deity was proven again   John 6
as a crowd of five thousand was fed.
He increased a young lad's meager lunch
to multiple baskets of fish and bread!

This inspired His teaching of the true bread as
the crowds sought more miracles from Him:
"I am the bread of life, He said. He who
comes to Me will never hunger again!
Anyone who comes to Me, I will
by no means cast away.
Everlasting life will be his; I will
raise him up the last day!"

***

An adulteress woman was brought to Jesus   John 8
as He was teaching in the temple one day.
The scribes and Pharisees were testing
Jesus to see what He might say:
"She should be stoned!" they cried.
"It's what Moses's law commands!"
But Jesus slowly answered,
"Let him who is without sin, pick
up the first stone in his hands!"

One by one they fled in guilt as
they came to the realization
Jesus understood their hearts and motives—
He had reversed the situation!
Turning to the woman, Jesus said, "They
have gone—those who accused you before.
Neither do I condemn you; go and sin no more.
Put the darkness behind, and true light
you will find when you follow Me.
For I am the Light of the world!"

***

In speaking with the Pharisees at   John 10
another time, Jesus declared,
"I am the Good Shepherd and the door to
the fold. All sheep must enter by Me.
I know My sheep; they hear My
voice, and they follow only Me.
I lay down My life that they might have
life and have it more abundantly!
Other sheep I have not of this fold,
My Father will give to Me.
No one can snatch the sheep I have;
in God's hand safe they will be.

David of old looked to the Lord as his Shepherd
while he cared for his flocks on the hill.   *Psalm 23*
Our empty souls crave guidance, protection,
and comfort that only our Shepherd can fill.

Jesus continued teaching His disciples   Matthew 16
as they traveled from place to place.
One day, in the region of Caesarea Philippi,
He questioned them face-to-face,
"Who do men say I, the Son of Man, am?"

"Some say John the Baptist, Elijah,
Jeremiah, or one of the prophets of old."

Jesus persisted with His question
until His real identity was told,
"But who do_you say that I am?"

As Peter heard the question,
his lips were unsealed.
"You are the Christ, Son of the living God!"
he spoke as to him it was revealed.

Jesus answered, "I say to you, that you are Peter
and on this rock My church I will build.
The gates of Hades shall not prevail against
it—My church will never yield!"

This same question Jesus asked is also asked of us:
"Who do you say I am?" and answer it we must!
We may try to ignore it, dodge it, or dismiss
it, but an answer we must proclaim.
For eternal life, life beyond death, is promised
only through our belief in His name!   *Acts 4:12*

***

Peter, James, and John accompanied
Jesus to a mountaintop one day.
Jesus was transfigured before
them as He began to pray.
His face shone like the sun; his
clothing was as white as light.
The disciples were astonished at   Matthew
this extraordinary sight!   17:1–9

Then Moses and Elijah appeared, and
with Jesus they spoke. Suddenly, a cloud
overshadowed them like a cloak.
A voice from the cloud sounded,
"Listen to my beloved Son; in Him
I am pleased!" Immediately the
disciples fell to their knees!
But Jesus reached down and,
touching them, said,
"Fear not; tell this to no one until the
Son of Man has risen from the dead!"

***

Jesus received a message that His friend   John 11
Lazarus of Bethany was gravely ill.
Lazarus's sisters, Mary and Martha,
knew Jesus had the power to heal.
But Jesus did not go to Bethany until Lazarus
had died and was four days in the tomb.
When He arrived, He came with great
power—even death He would consume!

After Jesus prayed to His Father, He cried with
a loud voice, "Lazarus, come forth!" as the
crowds watched with anticipation and fear.
He who had died was brought to life again!
Still bound in his grave clothes,
Lazarus soon did appear!
Jesus proclaimed, "Loose him and let him go!"
The glory of God was displayed for all
by the One who loved Lazarus so!

Jesus Christ has the power to recreate
life—this power we cannot deny.
For He said, "I am the resurrection and the
life. He who believes in Me shall never die!"

Jesus took time for little children, blessing them   Matthew 19
as they came, reminding His disciples heaven
was for those who humbly acted the same.

A rich young ruler approached Jesus
to inquire about eternal life.
He sadly departed after Jesus
conversed with him.
Jesus's words had cut like a knife!
Although the young man had obeyed many laws,
his wealth came between him and the Lord.
The word of God is powerful and
sharper than any two-edged sword!   Hebrews 4:12

Jesus told his disciples that a camel
could go through the eye of a needle
with a greater amount of ease,
Than a rich man could enter the kingdom of
God, falling down before God on his knees.
The disciples were very astonished, as this
teaching from the Lord they received.
"Who, then can be saved?" they inquired.
"Who, then will ever believe?"
Jesus answer was, "With men this is quite
impossible, but with God all things are possible!"

Six days before the Passover, Mary   John 12
anointed Jesus with her costly perfume,
showering His feet before His death,
not saving it for the tomb.

The next day, crowds waited for Jesus;
He approached Jerusalem, riding
on a donkey's young colt.
"Hosanna! Blessed is the King
of Israel!" they shouted.   Zechariah 9:9
The Pharisees feared a power revolt!

When Jesus entered the temple, He   Matthew 21
was filled with indignation.   Psalm 69:9
His Father's house had become a Wall Street station!
He made a whip of cords to drive
the moneychangers out,
and amid their cries, they heard Him shout:
"My Father's house shall be a house of prayer!
You have reduced it to a den of thieves!"
Then the Jews asked Him for a
sign to show the authority
He had to do such things as these.
Jesus answered, "Destroy this temple,
and I'll raise it in three days."
It made no sense to them since it took forty-   John 2
six years to build it using man's ways.
It was His body, the temple, to which
Jesus referred; after He rose from the dead,
they'd remember what they'd heard.

Jesus taught His disciples the temple   Mark 13
itself would face destruction.
This puzzled His disciples and
cause them to question,
"When will this happen and how can we know?"
A glimpse into the future, Jesus
answer would show. "Nations will be
troubled, and wars will occur.
Natural disasters will bring trials
that you must endure.
You will face persecution, trial, and arrest,
but the Holy Spirit will give you answers
when you are put to the test. Families will be
divided; some will face death for My sake.
The sun and moon will darken;
powers in the heavens will shake!
The Son of Man with His angels
in the clouds will appear.
They will gather His own from
both far and near.
Heaven and earth may pass away,
but My word will forever stay!"

Jesus's answer was difficult for
them to understand.
"Take heed," He said, "that I have told
you all these things beforehand!"
Then He warned, "No man will
know the hour or the day—take heed,
be ready, watch, and pray!"

Jesus predicted His death and resurrection   John 12
and said, "Father, glorify Your Name!
I could ask You to save Me from this hour,
but it is for this purpose that I came!"
Then a voice from heaven sounded, "I have
glorified it and will glorify it again."
The crowd assumed it was thunder or
an angel who had spoken to Him.

Jesus said, "This message was for
your benefit, not Mine.
For the judgment of the world and
its prince, it is now time!
But I, if I be lifted up, will
draw all men unto Me."
The disciples could not understand;
"Lifted up? This Son of Man?
How could this ever be?"

Jesus continued, "A little while
longer the Light is with you.
Believe in the Light and become
sons of Light too!
If you do not believe, I do not judge
you, for to save is the reason I came.
But in the last days, these words will judge
you if you fail to believe in My name!"

***

On the first day of the week, the disciples   *Mark*
prepared for the Passover in the upper room.   *14:12–25*
When Jesus said one of them would betray
Him, their hearts were filled with gloom.
As He dipped the bread into wine and handed
it to Judas Iscariot, the disciples heard Him say,
"The time has come; do what
you will do; do not delay!"
Then turning, Jesus continued,
"This is My blood shed for many
and My body broken for you."
The old covenant was passing;
this covenant was new!

Jesus assumed the role of a slave as He   John 13
bent to wash His disciples' feet.
When He came to Simon Peter,
with opposition He did meet.
But He replied, "If I do not wash you,
you will have no part of Me!"

This was difficult for Peter, but
in a while he would see!
"You call Me Teacher and Lord, and
yes, each of these is My name.
If then, as Master, I wash your feet, to
each other you must do the same.
A new commandment I leave with you,
love one another as I have loved you.
For by loving one another, the world
will see that you are My disciples—
those God has given to Me."

To Simon Peter's promise to go with Jesus to
prison or even death, Jesus gave this reply,
"Before you hear a cock crow, Simon,
knowing Me, three times you will deny."

Jesus spoke of mansions in heaven: "I will   John 14
go there to prepare a place for you.
But I will come again and receive you to myself
that where I am, there you may be too!
I am the way, the truth, and the life; no one
comes to the Father except through Me.
These words I speak, I speak not
on my own authority.
Believe Me that I am in the Father
and the Father in Me."

Jesus continued to reveal that He
and the Father were One.
And promised that after He left this world,
great things in His name would be done.
But He would not leave them alone—
orphans, they would not be.
He would send His Spirit of Truth to
teach and "to help you remember Me."
The Spirit would convict the world of sin,
of righteousness and judgment too.
"He will glorify Me, take what is
Mine, and declare it unto you.
Soon you will understand all this,
and joy will replace your sorrow.
Let not your heart be troubled. My
peace I leave for tomorrow."

Jesus has given us power to continue
His work in our world today.
And who better to fulfill this than you
and I, by what we do and say?
Is the busyness in our lives, to gain
what the world sees as best,
Crowding out the life God gives—
one of peace and lasting success?

The disciples declared their belief in Him   John 16
and that He came from His Father above.
Because they believed, Jesus assured them that
by both Father and Son they were loved!
"In this world you will have tribulation; but
let your hearts be filled with jubilation—
for I have overcome the world!"

***

Jesus prayed to His Father: John 17

"The hour has come; glorify Your Son.
You have given me authority over all that
they may know the only true God is You.
Now, offering Myself to erase sin and death
will finish the work you gave Me to do.
Glorify Me together with Yourself,
with the glory I had with You!"

Jesus prayed for His disciples:

"I have shared Your word, and those
You have given to Me have believed.
Now, may My joy by them be received.
By Your truth may they be sanctified, and
evil influence by the enemy be denied.
As they here on the earth do remain, use
their voices Your truth to proclaim."

Jesus prayed for all who in the
future would believe:

"I pray that all who come to the truth
will be one; that the world might
believe You sent Me, Your Son.
Father, I desire that My glory they will also see,
I in them, and You in Me.
By Our oneness may Your love be
made known—the same love with
which You loved Me be shown."

The chief priests, scribes, and elders   Matthew
of the people assembled together.   26–27
To defeat Jesus was their plan.
For only thirty pieces of silver,
Judas Iscariot agreed to betray the Son of Man!

Later, Judas would regret the awful
deed which he had done that day.
He'd return the silver, admitting
innocent blood he did betray.
With that being done, Judas Iscariot
ended his life in his own way.
With the silver pieces, the chief
priests purchased Potter's Field.
The fulfillment of Jeremiah's
prophecy was now revealed.

Jeremiah
32:6–9

***

"O My Father, not my will; Your will be done."

Jesus led His disciples to the   Matthew 26
Garden of Gethsemane,
"My soul is overwhelmed with sorrow,
"Stay here, pray, and keep watch with Me."
Being in anguish, He knelt to pray.
He expressed His obedience in
the words He did say:
"Father, if it is not possible that this
cup be taken from Your Son,
I'll drink it. May Your will be done!"

Two times Jesus found His disciples asleep.
Warning them, He said, "Watch   John 18
and pray; the spirit is willing
but the body is weak!"
The third time, He said, "Rise, the hour is near.
Come, let us go. My betrayer is here."

Troops led by Judas made their
way to Gethsemane.
"We seek Jesus of Nazareth!"
Jesus boldly proclaimed, "I am He!"

Peter drew his sword and cut off a servant's ear.
But Jesus quickly healed him as
He addressed Peter's fear,
"Should I not drink the cup My
Father has given Me?"
Then, turning to the officers, said,
"Take whom you came for;
let the others go free!"

The disciples fled as Jesus was
bound and led away;
taken to the high priest that very day.
Three times Peter was asked if he was one of
Jesus's followers, to which he answered, "No!"
As he hung his head, realizing he
had denied his Lord thrice, off in the
distance he heard a cock crow!

Jesus was sent to Pilate, the governor   John 19
of Judea, for judgment, but Pilate
could "find no fault in Him."
Still, he released Barabbas as was demanded,
although robbery was his sin.
Jesus, who was guilty of nothing,
had taken Barabbas's place!
Scourged, beaten, and crowned with thorns,
Jesus met His accusers face-to-face.
"Crucify Him! Crucify Him!" was their cry.
Reluctantly, Pilate sentenced Him to die.

Bearing His own cross, Jesus was
led to the Place of the Skull.
There He was crucified—for you
and me He took the fall!

There, nailed to the cross, was "Jesus
of Nazareth, King of the Jews"—God's
Conquering Son! Nothing but love
itself could do what He had done!
He could have called ten thousand
angels to come to set Him free; but
He chose to die alone, crying,   Psalm 22:1
"My God, My God, why have You forsaken Me!" Matthew 27:46

There, on the ground, beneath the cross, soldiers
cast lots for His garments. (*They had no clue!*)
Jesus spoke of them and the
others when He said,
"Father, forgive them for they
know not what they do!"

There, by the cross, was Mary—bearing the
anguish and pain not experienced by another.   Luke 23
Jesus saw her and John standing close by and
said to the disciple, "Behold your mother."

There, on either side of the cross,
two criminals hung in shame.
But one was assured a place in heaven
when he called on Jesus's name!

Then Jesus said, "I thirst," knowing
His work was now done.
Finally, He uttered, "It is finished!"
The victory had been won!
He cried with a loud voice, "Into Your hands I
commit My Spirit!" as He took His final breath.
The temple veil was torn from top to
bottom at the moment of Jesus's death!   Matthew 27

The sun refused to shine, so
darkness covered the earth   Amos 8:9–10
from the sixth to the ninth hour.
Earthquakes caused the rocks to split;
graves were unearthed as a result of the power.

The crowd of witnesses beat their breasts in fear!
"Truly this was the Son of God!"
exclaimed the centurion standing near.

No bones of Jesus were broken,
just as prophecy said;   Psalm 34:20
for when they looked at Jesus,
He was already dead.
But Jesus was pierced; water and blood
flowed freely from His side.   Zechariah
All our sins were washed away   12:10
with that crimson tide!

"Greater love hath no man than to
give His life for another."   *John 15:13*
I am released from the debt that I owe!
Oh, the height, the depth, the length and breadth—   *Romans 8:38*
no other love like this I'll know!

Jesus's death may appear to be a
defeat, but the opposite is true.
Although beaten by the powers of His day,
Jesus accomplished what He had come to do!
With His sacrifice, He "crushed the
serpent's head" in fulfillment of what
His Father, the Lord God, had said!   *Genesis 3:15*

On the cross He was triumphant,
though evil closed in.   *Colossians 2:15*
Refusing to retaliate, with good
He had overcome all sin!   *Romans 12:21*
The victim was the victor who arose and ascended!
The chasm between God and His
creation had now been mended!

***

That evening, Joseph of Arimathea and
Nicodemus prepared Jesus's body for the grave.
Bound with clean strips of linen, in a
new tomb, the body of Jesus was laid.
Women followed after him the
place of His burial to learn.
With spices and fragrant oils
later they would return.

The door of the tomb was covered as
a great stone was rolled in place.
Chief priests and Pharisees requested a
guard—just in case His disciples would steal
the body and claim He arose from the dead.
For, "In three days, I will rise!" was the
statement they recalled he had said!

***

On the first day of the week, an angel descended,   Matthew 28
rolled the stone from the door, and
waited for the women to appear.
His countenance was like lightning,
his clothing white as snow!
The guards were frozen with fear!

Mary Magdalene, Mary the mother of James,
and other women came upon the scene.
When they saw the tomb was open,
they were greatly perplexed!
In awe they gazed at the angel, wondering
whatever would come next!

The angel assured the women, "Don't be afraid.
Jesus, who was crucified is risen!
Come see where He was laid.
Now, go tell His disciples that
He is no longer dead.
You will see Him in Galilee for
He's already gone ahead."

In wonder and great joy, the
women started on their way.
They soon encountered Jesus;
"Rejoice!" they heard Him say!
They fell to the ground in worship,
their hands grasping at His feet.
"Don't cling to Me now, but go tell My
brethren in Galilee we will meet!"

***

The guards soon reported what had happened,
and the chief priests assembled
to decide what to do.
Deception and bribery were their plans
when their meeting together was through.
"Here, take this money. Tell them, 'As we
slept, His disciples stole Him away!'"
This plan to conceal Jesus's resurrection
is still repeated today.

***

Upon reaching the others, the women's   John 20
claims were met with unbelief.
But Peter and John, when they heard,
were curiously aroused from their grief.
Running quickly to the tomb, they
saw only grave cloths did remain.
Neatly folded by itself was the cloth from
Jesus's head, colored with the bloodstain!

***

Jesus appeared to His disciples,
saying, "Peace be to you!"
He showed His hands, His feet, and broke bread
with them to prove all they were seeing was true!
Thomas, one of the twelve, was
not among them that day.
When told they had seen Jesus, Thomas
doubted what they had to say.
Eight days later, Jesus came to them again.
"See my hands; believe!" He said to Thomas.
"Put your fingers in my side."
Thomas saw and believed.
"My Lord and my God!" Thomas cried.

Jesus again showed Himself to His disciples   John 21
as they dined on fish by the sea.
He restored Peter when He asked three times,
"Simon, son of Jonah, do you love Me?"
Peter's answers were always, "Yes,
Lord, You know I love you."
Jesus's instructions: "Then, tend and
feed My sheep; feed My lambs too."
Jesus explained the scriptures to his
disciples, helping them to comprehend
that this message of redemption would
go on—it would never end!

For forty days Christ was seen by   Acts 1
over five hundred brethren, proving
His resurrection was true.
During this time, He spoke with
His disciples, saying,
"As My Father has sent Me, I also send you."
To all nations, they were commissioned to preach
salvation in His name but told to wait until they
received power when the Holy Spirit came.

*Soon He would depart, leaving this group
to start a movement like no other—the
propagation of the Christian gospel from
man to man, from sister to brother.
This could be seen as "mission impossible,"
if you thought of it in human terms.
But the Holy Spirit would accomplish it
through them; their acts and transformed
personalities His power confirms!*

As Jesus lifted up His hands and blessed
them, He ascended in a cloud.
Two white-robed men appeared beside
them and spoke these words aloud:
"Why do you gaze into the heavens? This
same Jesus who was taken up from you
will come again in like manner when
God's work on earth is through."

*When Jesus left, the apostles must have felt
deserted and filled with great sorrow.
But they gathered together, wept, and prayed,
preparing for the promised power.
A vessel must be emptied before it can be filled.
Waiting upon God can be of great
value, it can give us time to yield.*

***

On the day of Pentecost, Jesus's followers   Acts 2
gathered together in one place.
Suddenly the sound of a mighty rushing
wind filled their entire space!
Tongues of fire appeared and rested
on each one, gracing them with the
ability to speak in another tongue!

This was witnessed by Jewish men
from every nation who were amazed
and perplexed at what they heard.
These followers of Christ were speaking of
the wonders of God in their own languages
so they could understand every word!
They questioned, "What does this mean?
Are they drunk with new wine?"
Peter rebuked them, quoting the
prophet Joel's words—   Joel 2:28–32
the promise of the coming of the
Spirit was of God's design.

Man's cooperative effort long ago to   *Genesis 11:1–9*
build a tower to reach heaven
was seen by God as rebellion at its worst!
When God divided man by confusing
their language, it must have seemed
as if they'd been cursed.
But now, here on Pentecost Day, what had
happened at Babel was for a time reversed!
In their own languages, men from all nations
heard God's plan for His church—the first!

The Holy Spirit had changed Peter, weak
and frightened, into "Peter the Rock"!
After the Spirit came upon him, he rose up   Acts 2
before the crowd, ready to "feed the flock."
Peter's words about Jesus, who was "put
to death but raised again for you,"
cut to his listener's hearts as they asked, "Men
and brethren, what shall we now do?"
Peter's answer, "Repent and be
baptized in Jesus's name.
Receive the Holy Spirit, whom
you witnessed as He came.
This promise is yours and also to all, as
many as the Lord our God will call."

Three thousand believers were added to
the church that first Pentecost Day.
They continued to meet together to
fellowship, break bread, and pray.
The believers sold their possessions,
sharing all they had as one.
As Jesus had promised, many signs and
wonders by the apostles were done.   John 14
They expressed their gladness and
praised their God above.
The Lord added daily to the church
all those who believed in His love.

***

At the gate of the temple, Peter and John　　　　　Acts 3–8
met a man who had been lame since birth.
He was asking for alms, not realizing God would
give him something of far-greater worth.
Peter said, "I offer you something greater
than silver, greater than gold!
In the name of Jesus, rise up and walk!"
The man was strengthened as he leaped
to his feet—no longer a victim of fate!
The amazed crowd followed Peter and
John to the portico just inside the gate.

This miracle of healing had
now opened the door.
Peter spoke to the crowd, many of
whom had denied Jesus before.
The message of the cross and Christ's
resurrection from Peter they now received;
the gospel's power reached to their core,
and five thousand men believed!

But the rulers of the temple
arrested Peter and John—
their preaching of the resurrection
they could not condone.
Brought before the Sanhedrin, Peter,
filled with the Spirit, reproved them,
"You have rejected Jesus, the chief cornerstone!　　　Psalm 118:22
There is no other name under heaven
by which salvation can be received!"

The rulers marveled at Peter's and
John's boldness; their connection
to Jesus they perceived.
They released them but warned them to
this instruction they must comply:
"Do not preach in the name of Jesus!"
To this, John and Peter did reply,
"We cannot listen to you; our
Lord we will not deny!"

When they left, they met with their companions;
together they raised their voices in one accord,
"Lord, look on these threats and grant
us your boldness that we may continue
to speak forth Your word."

The church went forward with
great purity and power.
Converts were added hour by hour.
Up to this point, the church
was pure—without sin,
but Ananias and Sapphira allowed
Satan an entry, and sin crept in.
They paid for their deception
with their very own lives.
In this holy atmosphere, sin could not survive!

The apostles continued preaching in Jesus's name
and healing great multitudes as they came.
The high priest was filled with much indignation;
how dare they preach Christ
against his stipulation!

To arrest and imprisonment, the
apostles were subjected.
But God had another plan—His word and
His messengers would be protected!
That night, an angel appeared and
opened the prison door.
His message to them:
"Go stand in the temple, and teach the
words of life as you have done before!"

When confronted, the apostles said it was
God they must obey, for they were Jesus's
witnesses since that crucifixion day.
The authorities listened to Gamaliel,
a teacher of the law,
"I advise you to set these men free; if they are
not of God, they will fail; but if they are of God,
no man—not even you—will ever, ever prevail!"

Stephen, a Godly man, one of great merit,
was chosen as a deacon. He was
filled with the Spirit.
There arose some who came against
Stephen; they stirred up controversy
and finally seized him.

He was brought before the council
to defend his situation.
He spoke the truth with power and
authority, much to their aggravation.
He recalled the history of the Israelite
nation, how God had kept and delivered
them through much tribulation.
He spoke honestly about how,
against God, Israel rebelled.
Facts he exposed, which they
thought they had quelled.
He called them "stiff-necked" as they
also were resisting God's Spirit.
When he gazed toward heaven, saying he saw
Jesus at the right hand of God, they could
tolerate no more—they wouldn't hear it!

They rushed together to seize him;
they would cast him out!
But as they began to stone him, they
heard Stephen loudly shout,
"Lord Jesus, receive my spirit, but do
not charge them with this sin."
A young man named Saul held the cloaks
of those as they hurled the stones at him.

***

The persecution of the Jerusalem church
caused its members to be scattered.
But wherever they went, they spread the gospel;
this was their life; this was what mattered!

Philip, the first evangelist, conducted
a soul-winning crusade.
Many in the city of Samaria believed what
they heard; they confessed, and were saved.
Guided by the Spirit, Philip
instructed an Ethiopian man in the
knowledge of Jesus, God's Son.

The gospel was shining its light, breaking through
boundaries; foreign missions had now begun.

***

Now Saul, who was present at Stephen's death,   Acts 9
was on his way to Damascus,
more Christians to retrieve.
He was fervent in his persecution of the
Jews who had chosen to believe.
Saul was a total unbeliever in Christ as
the Messiah and acted with great zeal.
He was learned in Jewish law, even
studying under the great Gamaliel.

But Saul would meet Jesus Christ, and
his life would be completely reversed:
Unknown to him, he would bear Christ's
name—the name which before he had cursed.
He would preach salvation to the Gentiles,
from whom before he'd have fled.
No longer inflicting pain on Christians,
Saul would endure perils and
suffering for Christ instead.

On his journey to Damascus, a light shone
from heaven so bright Saul couldn't see.
He fell to the ground as he heard a voice saying,
"Saul, Saul, why are you persecuting Me?"

"Who are you, Lord?" Saul questioned.

"I'm Jesus—the one whom you are trying
to defeat! Arise, go to the city and wait.
For further instructions there's a
man that you must meet!"

The men traveling with Saul were speechless;
they'd heard a voice, but no person could
they find! Helped to his feet, Saul opened
his eyes and realized he was now blind!
He was led to Damascus, held by his hand.
For three days he neither ate nor drank
but waited for the Lord's command.

In Damascus, the disciple Ananias
received word from the Lord,
"Find Saul, and restore his sight."
"Lord," Ananias replied, "this man
has done harm to all of your saints;
am I hearing you right?"
But Ananias was assured by the Lord
that this was meant to be.
"Saul is a chosen vessel of Mine; he'll
bear My name; he'll suffer for Me."

Ananias went on his way to find
Saul just as he had been told.
Laying his hands on him, he said, "Brother
Saul, the Lord Jesus, who met you on the
road, directed me to come to the house
of Judas, where I would find you.
Now receive your sight at this very moment
and be filled with the Spirit too!" Immediately
something like scales fell from Saul's eyes!
With both physical and spiritual sight
received, he arose and was baptized!

***

Saul soon bore witness of his new faith in Christ.
He spoke in the synagogues of
Damascus about his changed life.
Former Jewish friends became his
enemies; to kill him was their plan!
But God provided a way out; He had a
greater purpose for this man! Concealed in
a basket and let down through the wall,
Saul escaped their plot to kill him,
for he had just begun God's call.

God raised up Barnabas to become
Saul's Christian friend.
Barnabas brought Saul before the other apostles;
to them, his conversion Saul would defend.

***

Peter also continued in his ministry; by
his miracles the church was edified.
Walking in the fear of the Lord and comfort
of the Spirit, the church was multiplied.

God moved Peter's heart through visions,   Acts 10–15
preparing him to accept Gentiles
to the faith as well as Jews.
Peter was sent to the home of Cornelius, a
centurion, to preach of Christ's good news.
Peter perceived that God was not
partial; the word God sent through
Israel was that God was Lord of all!
Cornelius's household believed the message
of Jesus; on them the Spirit did fall!

Returning to Jerusalem, Peter had his own
Jewish brethren with which to contend.
He spoke of his vision and his
visit to Cornelius, revealing that to
Gentiles, God's grace did extend.
They were silenced when they were
told of all that had occurred.
Then they began praising their merciful
God as they understood Peter's word.

***

Being instructed by the Holy Spirit, Saul and
Barnabas received their first missionary call.
Preaching to the Gentile nations
would require giving their all!
Cyprus, Barnabas's native land,
would be their first stop.
It was during this time Saul became Paul,
as his Greek name he did adopt.
Then on to Pisidia, Iconium, Lystra, and Derbe.
Paul and Barnabas faced persecution and
abuse in each town on their journey.
But some became believers as Christ
crucified was faithfully preached.
Through Paul's Spirit-filled messages,
both Jews and Gentiles were reached.

***

Paul and Barnabas returned to the church
to aid in an important decision,
whether Gentiles needed to obey all
Jewish laws was causing a division.
It was decided they would be admitted to the
church as they followed Christ's commands.
The prophet Amos foretold that Gentiles,
too, were part of a loving God's plans.   Amos 9:11–12

***

Paul took Silas on his second missionary journey.   Acts 16–17
Together they revisited the churches
that had been started before.
As the converts were nurtured in their faith,
their numbers increased more and more.

They journeyed on to Macedonia
after receiving a vision.
Here they witnessed to Lydia;
to believe and be baptized was her decision.

To the great Greek cities of Philippi,
Thessalonica, Athens, Corinth, and Ephesus,
Paul, Silas, and Timothy took
the witness of their Lord.
Again, they faced both rejection and acceptance,
as they continued instructing in God's word.

Paul and Silas were beaten and imprisoned
for casting an evil spirit from a girl in Philippi.
At midnight they were praying and
singing hymns to God, as the jailers
and other prisoners listened nearby.

Suddenly the foundations of the prison were
shaken as a great earthquake did occur.
The Philippian jailer was about to
kill himself, for he had been charged
with keeping them secure.
Paul called out, "Do not harm yourself,
for we have not fled!" When he saw this
was true, the jailer fell to his knees.
"What must I do to be saved?" he said.

"Believe on the Lord Jesus Christ,
and you will be saved, and your household too!"

The jailer took them to his house and
washed the stripes they had received.
After hearing the word of the Lord from
Paul, he and his whole family believed.

In Thessalonica, Paul went to
the synagogue of the Jews.
For three Sabbath days, he reasoned
the scriptures with them to inform
them of God's good news.
He gave evidence that it was necessary for
the Christ to suffer and rise from the dead.
"This Jesus I am proclaiming to you
is Christ the Messiah," he said.
Some Jews were persuaded to join
Paul and Silas, as well as many Jewish
proselytes who were Greek.
But some unbelieving Jews became jealous; these
"troublemakers," Paul and Silas, they would seek.

Hidden by the brethren in the day, Paul
and Silas left in the middle of the night.
In Berea, they again won many converts
until the Jews from Thessalonica discovered
them and came to continue their fight.

Paul was sent on to Athens; he'd
wait for his companions there.
But as he looked around this great
city, he was filled with despair.
He saw the city had been given over to idols;
statues of false gods were everywhere.
So he began to hold discussions in the Jewish
synagogue and every day in the public square.

Greek philosophers requested he come to the
Areopagus to present his doctrinal view.
For the Athenians were known for spending
their time debating anything new.
Paul spoke of their altar inscribed
"To the Unknown God."

"The One whom you worship without
knowing, Him, I proclaim to you!"
As they listened, they heard about
the "Man ordained by God."
But they questioned whether
the resurrection was true.
Some mocked, "Another time we'll need to hear
about this; our conversation is not through!"

***

Paul went on to Corinth, where   Acts 18
he met Aquila and Priscilla,
who had been ordered along with
other Jews to leave Rome.
They were tentmakers just as he was, so he
helped them while staying in their home.
Every Sabbath, he preached about Jesus
until the Jews began to resist.
"Your blood be on your own heads," Paul
said, "if in darkness you choose to exist!"
Paul would take his witness to the Gentiles.
No doubt he felt failure and was grieved.
But Crispus, ruler of the synagogue,
had heard Paul's message.
He and his entire household believed!

The Lord reassured Paul of his safety in a vision.
God would use the proconsul Gallio
to silence Jewish opposition.
There were many more people in
Corinth whom Paul was yet to reach.
So he stayed in that city a year and a half,
affecting many lives as he continued to preach.

Then Paul and his friends Aquila
and Priscilla sailed for Syria.
Stopping at Ephesus, he was requested to stay.
Since Paul was determined to
keep the feast in Jerusalem,
he promised he'd return to them another day.

On his third missionary journey,   Acts 19-26
Paul again revisited the churches
he had already begun.
He returned to Ephesus as he had promised.
There, many converts to Christ were won.

God worked unusual miracles by the hands of
Paul: diseases were cured, evil spirits exorcised,
and books of magic burned before all!
The word of the Lord prevailed and grew.   Isaiah
But as usual, the adversary was active too.   55:10–11

A riot occurred when shrines made to the
goddess Diana were no longer in demand.
Demetrius and his fellow craftsmen were
not making the income they had planned.
But the clerk of Ephesus hushed the
crowd; this riot was not without flaw.
"It seems there is no real reason for this
commotion against these men; if there
is, bring it to the court of law."

As Jewish plots against Paul increased, he
departed for Troas, leaving Greece.
Paul joined his companions, breaking bread
and ministering to them well into the night.
A young man named Eutychus,
seated on a window ledge, fell asleep
and took a three-story flight.
Though he died upon hitting the
ground, Paul raised him to life again.
When morning dawned, the people took
Eutychus home, greatly rejoicing with him.

Paul felt called by the Spirit to go to Jerusalem,
surmising in time he'd face suffering and strife.
But joyfully finishing the race for which
God had called him, was a goal more
important to Paul than his life!
Along the way, he was warned by
friends of the danger that awaited.
But Paul felt strongly he needed to go;
he could not be otherwise persuaded.
He reminded them of all he had given—
that it was better to give than receive.
"Be on your guard; shepherd the
flock; know what you believe!
There will be those who will distort
the truth to try to lead you astray.
I never stopped warning you of this
for years both night and day."
Tears were shed; goodbyes were said;
they knew they'd not see him again.
Then on to Jerusalem Paul continued,
to face what was willed for him.

In Jerusalem, Paul attempted to make peace
with the Jews, but peace was not to be found.
Accusing Paul of disregarding their law, they
seized him; with two chains he was bound.
Before the crowd, Paul was allowed to speak—to
tell of his life and spiritual transformation.
But sadly, the Jewish mob's mentality was
focused only on Paul's annihilation.

Claiming his Roman citizenship,
Paul was protected
and whisked away in the middle of the night.
But not before the Lord spoke, "You have
witnessed for me in Jerusalem, Paul; now
in Rome, you will also give light."

Held as a prisoner, Paul was now brought to
trial when he received Governor Felix's call.
The high priest Ananias and his lawyer had
come with the case they prepared against Paul.
Paul's rebuttal denied proof of any of the
charges brought against him on that day.
"I worship the God of our Fathers
as a follower of the Way.
I incited no riot, gathered no crowds, only
came with gifts for the poor," he said.
"No disagreement should there be, unless it is
that I spoke of the resurrection of the dead."

Felix scheduled his judgment of
Paul's case for a later day.
Meanwhile, he called for Paul frequently
to hear what he had to say.
Paul witnessed of his faith in Christ
and told of coming judgment too.
This frightened Felix, who announced,
"Your discourse now is through!
When I find it more convenient,
I'll be sure to send for you."

After two more years, Felix
was replaced by Festus,
to whom the Jews again presented their case.
Saved from the Jews by appealing to Caesar,
Paul witnessed to Festus and
King Agrippa face-to-face.
So powerful were Paul's words,
so intriguing and so bold,
King Agrippa admitted, "Almost, I am
persuaded at what I have been told!"

Those who were in authority realized   Acts 27–28
Paul was guilty of no crime.
But since Paul appealed to Caesar, his
case would be heard one more time.
So Paul would go on to Rome
instead of being set free.
Paul, his centurion guard, and other prisoners
boarded the ship, which set out to sea.

Not much progress was made on the journey
as the winds were exceedingly strong.
Paul warned, "Men, I perceive, if we
continue this voyage, all will definitely go
wrong! Disaster awaits for the ship and
its cargo, as well as all life on board."
But the centurion followed the advice of
others rather than trusting Paul's word.

So they continued on their journey,
thinking that the worst of the weather
was through; but soon they would
discover that the opposite was true!
The ship, by tempestuous winds, was tossed!
After days of seeing neither the sun nor
the stars, any hope of a rescue was lost!
Throwing much off the ship, they lightened
the load; food rations barely met their need.
It was then Paul reminded them of his
warning which they had failed to heed;
"But now take heart to what I have to say!
An angel of the God to whom I belong has
assured me of my safety, as well as all of you.
We will run aground on an island;
only the ship will be lost.
So take heart, men, for I believe
all God has told me is true!"

On the fourteenth night, as the ship
was still being tossed along the way,
Paul advised the men to eat; they would
need strength for their next day.
As an example to all two hundred
seventy-five men on board,
Paul broke bread and ate, offering
thanks to his Almighty Lord.

When daylight appeared, they saw a bay
having what looked like a beach.
Hoisting the main sail, they headed
that way, hoping land to reach.
But the ship was grounded and remained
unmovable, firmly stuck in the sand.
Everyone jumped overboard in obedience
to the centurion's command.
The ship was broken up by the violence of
the waves; but as Paul had promised, not
a man was lost—everyone was saved!

On the island of Malta they were welcomed by
the natives who built a fire to keep them warm.
As Paul gathered sticks to add to the fire, a
viper came out and attached to his arm!
The natives all believed Paul must be a god,
when they witnessed that it did him no harm!

Governor Publius of Malta gave hospitality
to Paul and company for several days.
When his father fell ill, Paul visited him,
placed his hands on him, and prayed.
News of the father's healing spread,
and as the islanders heard, many with
diseases came to receive Paul's prayers
and were miraculously cured!
In turn, the islanders honored them greatly,
so when they were about to depart, they
loaded the ship with all they would need—
gifts of kindness straight from their heart.

***

Their first stop was Puteoli, where Paul met
Christian brothers and remained for seven
days. Arriving at Rome Paul was encouraged by
more friends for whom he gave God praise.

In Rome, Paul was allowed to live by himself
and soon called together the leaders of the Jews.
"It is for the hope of Israel, I'm
bound with this chain."
They agreed to hear Paul's views.
From morning till evening, he explained
the Kingdom of God, trying to
convince them of Jesus as he taught
from Moses's Law and the prophets.
Some Jews believed; others disagreed.
But when Paul quoted Isaiah,
they took their leave.   Isaiah 6:9–10
"You will ever be hearing but not understanding;
ever seeing, but never perceive.
For this people's hearts have become hardened.
They refuse to turn, be healed and pardoned."

Paul remained in Rome, teaching the
Gentiles and all who would hear.
He fulfilled his purpose to speak boldly
about Jesus for two additional years.

Although we know Christ had ascended,
we see His presence was extended;
In the book of Acts, His Spirit worked
through His chosen few.
Today Christ's Spirit lives through His followers.
His acts, He continues to do.

***

The Holy Spirit's breath of inspiration is
evident in Paul, a gifted vessel for God's use.   *2 Timothy 3:16*
Paul wrote letters to the churches, gracing
them with additional spiritual truth.
His desire was to continue teaching and
encouraging them by what the Spirit led him to say.
For he knew they would face persecution as
evil would seek to obstruct their way.

In his letter to the Romans, Paul   Romans 1–8
shared the gospel without shame,
for he knew it is the power of salvation
for all who believe in Christ's name.
The good news is that through our
Redeemer, from sin we can all be healed.
For it is by faith we are justified as the
righteousness of God is revealed.

Paul confirms all creation bears the
fingerprints of our God—
of His wisdom, His power, and His glory.
Man's problem is not lack of
evidence but rejection of truth, in
favor of his own desired story.
Instead of honoring and thanking God
for His revelation, man chose to serve
himself above the God of all creation.

Paul says we must not judge or blame
others, for we also are guilty of sin.
Let us not be like Adam, who blamed Eve,
or Eve saying of the serpent, "It was him."
God's kindness is to lead us to repent
and to live a life that's pure.
But if we are self-seeking and reject His truth,
God's anger and wrath we'll endure.
All will be judged by our righteous God.
His laws have been inscribed on each heart.   *Ecclesiastes 3:1*
Our inner urge to do good and our guilt when we
choose to do wrong confirms God has done His part.

Truth revealed but truth rejected, deserves
God's judgment—His righteous indignation.
But how great was the love of our dear Savior,
offering His life to heal our separation!

All have sinned; all are guilty
ever since the fall of man.
But by God's grace, the free gift of redemption
is available through God's plan.

How are we justified? How do
we righteousness obtain?
Is it by obeying the law or doing good?
No, these are one and the same.
Abraham was credited with righteousness
because he had faith God's promises were true.
He'd become the "father of many nations,"
for that's what God said He'd do.
Paul says we, too, are counted as righteous
if we believe the promise that was given
to us in our helpless situation.
We must believe God delivered
Jesus to death and raised Him to life
again for our sanctification.

Through one man's offense judgment came
to all men, resulting in condemnation.
But in another Man's righteous act, all
who believe receive justification.
When we are justified by faith, we have peace
with God, knowing that Christ took our place.
The punishment we deserve because of
our sin, we now no longer must face!

If man continues in his sin, he will
collect sin's wages—eternal separation,
no chance to be set free.

But if man accepts God's gift
through Jesus Christ,
He'll cast all our sins into the depths of the sea!   Micah 7:19

We are then dead to sin but alive in Christ;
from our slavery we've been set free!
We are not under law but under grace—
servants of our righteous God are we!
The gift of God is eternal life!
Who could ask for anything more?
This is a promise of unending life with our
triune God, as had been intended before!

Paul teaches God gave the law as a guide to life   Galatians
until faith came—a tutor to bring us to Christ.   3:19–25
Although the law is and was good,
it cannot save us from our sin.
In His love and mercy, God chose to do
what the law cannot do for men.
Jesus fulfilled the righteous
requirements of the law.   1 Corinthians
His life was free of sin—perfection!   5:21
He took life's cycle of sin and death
and brought it under subjection!

OMWG OH, MY WONDERFUL GOD!

If we have chosen Christ as our Savior
and are walking in His Spirit,
there is no condemnation—
no more reason to fear it!
We receive the Spirit of adoption;
"Abba, Father," we proclaim.
The Spirit testifies with our spirit;
"God's child" is our new name.
Because we are adopted as God's children,
we are co-heirs with His Son!
Both His sufferings and His
glory we will share as one!
Suffering in this present world will not
compare to the glory yet to be.
All creation now waits in expectation
from its bondage to be set free!

Paul is confident that neither life nor death,
nor things present nor things to come,
no powers on earth nor in heaven
above can separate us from God's
love, in Jesus Christ His Son!

Paul shares his great sorrow and   Romans 9–16
continual grief that to the law
his own countrymen are yet enslaved.
Paul's desire and prayer is that they
submit to the righteousness of God in
Christ and thereby would be saved.
His says his own have a zeal for God
but not according to knowledge.
For the heavens have declared the glory of God;
day and night, knowledge has been revealed.
Yet a portion of Jews, though not
all, have rejected the Messiah,
refusing to turn and be healed.
There is no distinction between Jew and
Greek; the same Lord is Lord over all.
He is rich in mercy to any who in
humility respond to Christ's call.

But Paul asks, "How can they call
on Him if they don't believe?
And how can they believe if they haven't heard?
And how can they hear without a
preacher presenting the word?"
For faith comes by hearing the gospel plan.
How beautiful is he who brings the good news!   Isaiah 52:7

How beautiful are the feet of that man!

Hear the call from Jesus while
He walked on this earth:

"Come unto Me, all you who
labor in your own strength,
under the heavy load of sin,
and I will give you rest.
Take My yoke upon you, learn from me. I'll
give you abundant life—life at its best! For
I am gentle. My heart is loving and kind.
My yoke is easy. My burden is light.
Come! True rest you will find!"

God is truly sovereign, and we are truly
accountable to accept His invitation.
If we confess with our mouth the Lord
Jesus and believe in our hearts
God raised Him from the dead,
we will receive salvation.

Paul persists in his teaching of God's
sovereignty and man's free will.
To understand fully the mind of God
is beyond our comprehension.
Paul uses the illustration of the vessel
made by a potter, having no power
to discern the potter's intention.
So it is with God's sovereign plan—it is
beyond the understanding of finite man!

Matthew
11:28–30

Through Israel's hardness of
heart toward the Messiah,
God's mercy was extended to
every Gentile nation.
Could this arouse Israel to jealousy
and lead to their salvation?
If by Israel's rejection, the world,
to reconciliation was led,
What more can their acceptance bring
but eternal life from the dead!

By God's grace, the Gentiles have been grafted
in as branches of the patriarchal olive tree.
They have replaced some of the original
branches that lost their identity.
But God in His rich mercy may graft them
in again, if they turn from their unbelief—
He's not forgotten His promises to them.

So we see the salvation of both Jews and
Gentiles depends on God's grace alone.
Neither can boast of achieving salvation by
any good thing they have done on their own.
God shows His kindness to those who respond
in faith to the sacrifice of Jesus, His Son.
But God will show His justice to those who compete
with the cross, boasting in the works they have done.

God's riches, wisdom, and knowledge
go deep—ever, so ever deep!
His judgments and ways are
far beyond man's grasp.
"Who can know the mind of God?" I ask.
What advice to God can mere man bring?
For from Him, to Him, and
through Him is everything!

Isaiah
40:13–14

Paul urges Roman believers to
offer themselves to God.
Their worship and loving service will make
it understood that the will of God is proven
to be acceptable, perfect, and good!
This can only happen as the human mind is
opened to the Spirit's transforming power—
not allowing the world to press them into
its mold *as it seeks to do so hour after hour*!

Paul warns them about thinking more
highly of themselves than they should.
"Use the gifts God has given you, love
sincerely, hate evil, desire what is good.
Bless those that persecute you;
do not take revenge.
For God has said, 'I will repay;   Deuteronomy
it is Mine to avenge!'   32:35
If your enemy is hungry, feed him; if
thirsty, give him something to drink.
In doing so, you will heap burning
coals upon his head.
*Shaming his evil with good could
possibly make him think!*

Submit to the authorities, whom God
has established, to rule over you.
Give them both honor and respect;
pay the taxes that are due.
Put aside deeds of darkness; put
on the armor of light.
Clothe yourselves with the Lord Jesus
Christ, not gratifying the desires of the
sinful nature but doing what is right.

Accept the one whose faith is weak;
pass no judgment on one another.
Make no stumbling block or obstacle
that could destroy your brother.
The kingdom of God is not a matter of eating
or drinking, but of peace and joy in the Spirit;
Accept one another, as Christ has accepted you.
For Christ became a servant to
demonstrate God's mercy to the Gentile
and confirm His promises to the Jew."

****

Paul had founded the Corinthian Church with
people who were formerly part of a pagan nation.
Coming from such darkness, they needed
instruction to grow in their salvation.
Paul admonished them to examine and correct their
ways as they were illuminated by Christ's light.
His letters are beneficial to all churches,
in all times offering spiritual insight.

Paul begins his letter to the   1 Corinthians
Corinthians thanking God   1–3
for His grace and His faithfulness
to them each day.
Because of their faith in Christ they
have been enriched in every way.
Now he pleads with them that the
divisions among them be replaced with
unity, allowing the power of the cross of
Christ to continue to set men free.

Paul's preaching of Christ was not by human
wisdom nor his own persuasive word; rather
by a demonstration of the Spirit's power,
God's message through him was heard.
The hidden wisdom of God that was
ordained before the present time is now
revealed through His Spirit—things beyond
understanding, magnificent, sublime!

Faith must not be in the wisdom of the
world but rather in God's power.
Paul admonishes them to grow up in
Christ—now is the time; now is the hour!
He instructs them to stop worrying
about whom they would follow.
The Lord had given men to minister
to them—Paul, and also Apollo.
We are all God's workers; we plant
and water the seeds of salvation.
But it is God who gives the increase
if Christ is the foundation.

"You are a temple in which God's Spirit dwells.   1 Corinthians
Take care," Paul warns, "to be faithful   5
and do not defile yourselves.
Abstain from sexual immorality,
thievery, covetousness, drunkenness,
extortion, and verbal abuse.
For participation in these unrighteous
acts is without excuse.
Glorify God in both your body and spirit,
so the Kingdom of God you may inherit."

Paul states that as an apostle, his   I Corinthians
life is lived in self-denial.   9–13
For the sake of the gospel, he suffers
much and endures much trial.
Though he is free, he becomes a slave to all,
hoping that in doing so, on Christ men will call.
The crown he seeks is an imperishable one; it
will be his reward when life's journey is done.

Paul reminds them to continue to remember
the Lord's Supper as they congregate;   1 Corinthians
"Before doing so, examine yourself that   11
you may be found worthy to partake."
Jesus took the bread and the cup of wine.
"This is my body, broken for you, this
cup, the new covenant in My blood.
Take this in remembrance of Me."
Whenever you eat the bread and drink the cup,
you proclaim His death till He comes in victory!

Paul explains that each of them is a
member of the body of Christ.
Each one has been given a spiritual gift.
Its use is to profit not one, but many.
In the physical body, is there
a part that's superior?
The answer to that is, "Not any"!
All gifts are given to make the body complete.
All gifts must work together
rather than compete.
Each gift is like a clanging cymbal,
if not accompanied with love.
Love, the very essence of God,
stands out far above.

Love is kind, patient, and forgiving.
In truth love does rejoice.
It is not proud, selfish, nor easily
provoked. Rudeness is not its voice!
Love will not fail; love will not cease to be.
Faith, hope, and love abide, but love
is the greatest of these three.

Paul emphasizes that the risen Christ
is the reason for all hope.
In Adam we all face death, but
in Christ we rise again!
If there had been no resurrection,
we all would remain in sin!
At Christ's second coming, the
final trumpet call will sound.
Our metamorphosis will occur—by corruption
and mortality, we'll no more be bound!
Death will have no victory;
death will have no sting.
We will from that time on bear the
image of our heavenly King!

1 Corinthians
15

***

In his second letter to the
Corinthians, Paul blesses God
for the comfort he has received
through all his tribulation.
He is thankful that wherever he
is led he is triumphant
as he diffuses the fragrance of
Christ—God's salvation.

2 Corinthians

He reminds the Corinthians that they are
his joy; he loves them as his very own.
For they are Christ's epistles, written on
tablets of flesh rather than tablets of stone.
Paul says the veil has been removed from
our eyes; the Spirit has set us free.
We continue to be transformed into His
likeness, as we reflect the Lord's glory.

Paul explains the light of Christ's gospel
is veiled to those who do not believe.
Satan, the god of this world, has blinded
them so the truth they do not perceive.
It is the God who said, "Let light shine
out of darkness," who gives us the light
to see that His glory is in the face of
Christ—the one who can set us free!

Though Paul is often cast down with afflictions,
he is not destroyed nor given to despair.
As he carries about in his body the
death of Jesus, so also, the life of Jesus
he knows that he will share.

Paul says, "Death may be working
in our outward man, but our inward
man is being renewed day by day.
These temporary afflictions are for the
moment; eternal glory, yet unseen,
will be coming our way!"

Our earthly bodies are like a tent—
our stay in them is temporary.
But we long for our heavenly habitat—
the one that is extraordinary!
Swallowed up by life our mortality will be.
This, God has promised; His
Spirit is our guarantee!

Since we walk by faith and not
by sight, let us make it our aim to
please God, to do what's right.
We'll come before Christ at the judgment
seat; our works will be judged by Him.
But because we are a new creation in
Christ, we'll not be judged for our sin.
For on the cross, Christ faced sin's condemnation;
our sin was canceled as we received His salvation.

Paul continues to tell the Corinthians to
come out from the darkness of unbelievers
and live for God, lives separated unto Him.
For what fellowship has light with   Jeremiah
darkness when God's promise   31:1, 9
was to dwell and to walk with them?

Paul says to remember the Lord Jesus—
though He was rich, He chose to become
poor; that through His poverty, His
followers would have riches far beyond
what they could have imagined before!
Christ's grace in giving should be our example
as we give to others in need.
Give out of the abundance of your heart.
God loves a cheerful giver indeed!

Paul warns against being fooled by Satan,
who poses as an angel of light.
"Use God's spiritual weapons," he says,
"as you continue the spiritual fight."
Paul fears the Corinthians may be ensnared
by a false gospel filled with deceit.
He admonishes them to grow in Christ,
striving to become complete.

Paul has experienced God's promise
in his own afflictions:
"My grace is sufficient for you; in your
weakness My strength is made known."
For this reason, Paul boasts in his weaknesses,
demonstrating that the source of his
strength comes from his God alone.

***

In Paul's letter to the Galatians, he clarifies	Galatians
that man is justified only by	
his faith in Jesus Christ.	
He says, "For it is written, 'Cursed is everyone	Deuteronomy
who does not perfectly follow the law.'"	27:26
Only Christ could save us because His life	
was perfect—without even a single flaw!	Deuteronomy
Christ became that curse for us;	21:23

He paid the price as He hung on Calvary's tree.	
The law was given to show our need	
of a Savior who could set us free.	Galatians 3:24

Paul says everything we do must in faith be done.	
For without faith it is impossible	Hebrews
to please the Holy One!	11:3–6
We are to walk in faith, as Enoch	Genesis
did in the story of long ago.	5:21–22

We are to pray in faith without doubt,
not as a wave tossed to and fro.   James 1:5–7
We are to understand by faith,
and by faith be filled.   Ephesians 5:18
The fiery darts of the evil one are
quenched, as faith becomes our shield.   Ephesians 6:16

Paul urges believers to walk in the Spirit—that
is, seek Him and let Him be your guide.
We'll not succumb to the desires of the
sinful nature if in Him we do abide!
The results of His Spirit in us will produce
these fruits, which all men do extol: unselfish
love, joy, peace, longsuffering, gentleness,
goodness, faith, and self-control.

                              ***

Paul's letter to the Ephesians is   Ephesians
one of doctrine and faith
to both them and succeeding generations.
He says God's adoption of us as
His sons and daughters,
He planned before earth's foundations.

"In Christ" and "in Him," these
words Paul says are key.
For in Him we begin, continue our
faith, and in Him our end will be!
Our redemption is in Christ; through
Him we've been set free.
When in faith we believe, we are sealed
with His Spirit as our guarantee!

Paul prays that his readers may be given
the spirit of wisdom and revelation,
to know the extent of their blessings
through the gift of His salvation.
How great is our hope!
How rich our inheritance now
and what still lies ahead!
The strength of the power working in us is the
same power that raised Christ from the dead!

By God's grace and our faith
salvation is God's gift to us,
not a gift we could either earn or demand.
Paul adds that we are created in Christ Jesus
for good works God prepared beforehand.

Christ is peace; He revealed God's mystery
and broke the wall of separation.
Both Jews and Gentiles are now one body
built on Christ as their foundation.

Be imitators of God; let Christ shine on you.
Make the most of every opportunity,
watching what you do.
Submit to one another out of
reverence to our Lord.
Children, obey your parents, as was
commanded in His word.
Evil powers will arise that you must fight against.
Use the armor of God as your sure defense.

***

To the Christians at Philippi, Paul shares   Philippians
his love and joy as he remembers them.
He is confident that God will continue His
work to make them complete in Him.
Paul writes from prison, saying his circumstances
have only furthered the gospel story. Whether
he lives or dies, his purpose is to magnify
Christ and give Him all the glory.
If he lives it will be for Christ; if
he dies it will be his gain.
He is confident he will visit them
so in the flesh he will remain.

Paul encourages the Philippians to
show their unity with Christ
by their humble care for one another.
He reminds them that in great humility
Christ gave up His position to
become their brother!
In obedience, death on the cross He
chose to face. Therefore, God has
exalted Him to the highest place.
To Him every knee will bow, every
tongue shall confess Him as Lord.
To God be all glory for grace!

Paul instructs, "Work out your
salvation as God is at work in you
both to will and to do His good pleasure.
In this perverse generation, hold fast to the
truth; as you shine forth your light, I rejoice.
You're my treasure!"

Paul advises, "Rejoice in the
Lord! Again, I say rejoice!
Be anxious for nothing; make
prayer your first choice.
His peace will flood your hearts and
minds as to God you lift your voice!"

Whatever is pure, noble, right, lovely, admirable,
praiseworthy, and true—thinking on things
such as these is what you should do.
As you put into practice the good that you
know, the God of peace will be with you!

***

Paul commends the Colossians for their faith and   Colossians
love, although he's not met them face-to-face.
He credits fellow minister Epaphras for
declaring to them God's truth and grace.
Paul continues to ground them in the full
revelation of Christ as he teaches—
By Him and for Him all things were created in
heaven and earth; over all things He is the head!
As God incarnate, Christ alone paid sin's debt,
making peace through His blood that was shed.
He is the very image of God, the head of the
church, and the firstborn from the dead.
Paul confirms their standing by declaring their
belief in Christ has resulted in their justification.
"Christ has reconciled you and presented you
holy, without a blemish, free of accusation.

Baptism, Paul says, symbolizes being buried in
Christ and raised in Christ, beginning life anew.
A resurrected life is one of seeking God's will
and being Christlike in all that you say and do.
In all your relationships, practice mercy and love.
Be thankful and prayerful to the Lord above.
Sing songs and hymns with grace in your
hearts to encourage your Christian brothers.
Let the word of Christ richly dwell in you
demonstrating a genuine faith to all others.

***

Paul writes to the Thessalonians, showing his   1 Thessalonians
tender affection for them as well as his concern.   1–5
He instructs them in their Christian walk,
as they wait for their Lord's return.
Paul says he and Silas came to them with the
gentleness of a mother and the exhortation
of a father, bearing the good news.
The Thessalonians welcomed and
received their message as the truth from
God rather than mere man's views.

He commends them for their further acts of
faith and love as witnessed by other men.
He assures them that "we will all rejoice in the
presence of Christ when He comes again."
Until that time, he instructs them to walk in
holiness as sons of the light, aware that the day of
the Lord will come as a thief comes in the night.

"Do not sorrow as others who have no hope,"
Paul teaches, "when a believer has passed away.
If you believe Jesus died and rose again, then
they also will rise and return with Him that day."
With trumpet sound and a shout from the
clouds, the Lord Himself will descend!
Believers on earth will be caught up with
them; all physical limitations will end!

Remember, God did not appoint us to wrath,
but that through Christ we'd receive salvation.
Our faithful God who called us, the God of
peace Himself, will complete our sanctification.
So while we wait, pray without ceasing,
test all things, and hold fast to the good.
Give thanks to God in everything,
knowing its God's will that you should.

***

In his second letter, Paul recognizes the   2 Thessalonians
persecution that the Thessalonians now face.   1–3
He states he is praying that God fulfill in them
the good pleasure of His grace. Concerning the
return of the Lord, Paul tells them of the events
to come, reassuring them that the Lord who
is faithful will guard them from the evil one.

He warns them against idleness, saying,
"Live an orderly life; work as you should."
He urges them to listen to his instructions
and to not grow weary in doing good.

***

Timothy was a younger companion of   1 Timothy 1–6
Paul, a helper and Christian brother.
As a boy, he had been instructed in scripture
by both a mother and grandmother.
Timothy, who was anointed to be an
evangelist, is now busy answering his call.
He receives insight and instructions for the
churches in letters from his mentor, Paul.

Paul begins his letter with a warning
that those who have strayed from
true doctrine must return.
For they have turned aside to idle talk, not
even understanding the things they affirm.
Paul charges Timothy to hold fast to the
faith; from a good conscience never waver.
Pray for all men, live a peaceful and reverent
life; for this is the will of our Savior.

That all men may come to the
knowledge of truth is God's plan.
Jesus, who ransomed us, is the one and
only mediator between God and man.

Paul gives instructions for conduct in
the church, with the emphasis that
"To their faith they remain true.
Don't let anyone despise your youth, Timothy;
don't neglect the gift prophetically given to you.
Instruct the brethren in godliness and to be
content with the provisions that they receive.
For we brought nothing into this
world and will take nothing with us
when it's time for us to leave!
Withdraw yourself from those who suppose
that godliness is a means of gain.
The love of money is a root of evil;
from greediness you must refrain."

Paul calls Timothy a "man of God,"
and charges him to guard that which
has been entrusted to his care.
"Teach the wealthy to be rich in good deeds,
to be generous and willing to share.
Fight the good fight of faith holding
on to eternal life; confess the Lord
Jesus Christ until He comes again.
For He alone is immortal, the Kings
of Kings and Lord of Lords!
To Him be all power and honor. Amen!"

Paul's farewell address demonstrates   *2 Timothy 1–4*
his spirit of triumph
as he awaits the Roman sword.
In a cold dungeon, Paul writes to Timothy that as
a good soldier of God, he's ready to reap his reward.

Paul tells Timothy, "Guard the precious
treasure that has been entrusted to you.
Use your God-given spirit of power, love,
and sound judgment in all you say and do.
Do not be ashamed of our testimony or my
chains; for I'm a prisoner of the Lord.
Be strong in the grace of God. Be diligent
as you rightly divide His word.
If we die with Christ, we shall
also live with Him.
If we endure, we shall also reign.
If we deny Him, He will deny us;
But if we are faithless, <u>His</u>
faithfulness will remain.

These are perilous times in which traitors will
preach a form of godliness but deny its power.
Continue in the scriptures, knowing they are
inspired by God to equip us for this hour.
I have fought the good fight; I
have finished the race.
I have kept the faith. The crown
of righteousness awaits me.
Our Lord is faithful and will deliver from
evil, until His heavenly kingdom we see!"

***

In his letter to Titus, Paul instructs the early   Titus 1–3
Christians as to what their lives should display.
By the grace of God they must live soberly,
righteously, and godly in the present day.
"Be subject to those in authority; be ready
to do what is good. Speak evil of no one;
show humility to all as you should.
God's mercy has saved you by the
washing of regeneration.
Having been renewed by the Spirit,
you're now a new creation."

***

While yet in prison, Paul continues to write.   Philemon
To Philemon, a member of the
church at Colosse, he appeals.
As he intercedes for a former slave, Onesimus,
a spirit of justice and kindness he reveals.
"When Onesimus returns to you,
treat him as you would treat me.
No longer a slave, he's a brother in
Christ, one who has been set free!"

***

The book of Hebrews is an exhortation for those
who might be drifting away from Christ— a
spiritual antidote prescribed for any day.
In New Testament times, some persecuted
Jewish Christians were unsteady in their faith;
they were in danger of losing their way.

In past times, God had spoken through prophets   Hebrews
but now speaks to mankind through His Son.
Christ is the image of God, the brightness of
His glory; *let's remember just what He has done.*

Through Christ, all the worlds were made
and upheld by the word of His power.
Coming to earth to purge us of
sin was His greatest hour.
Submitting to such great suffering and death,
Jesus Christ tasted death for everyone.
God crowned Him with glory and honor,
putting all things in subjection under His Son.
Now He is exalted higher than the angels,
sitting on the right hand of God on High.
How can we neglect so great a salvation;
how can we our Lord deny?

Jesus brings us, His sons and daughters, to
glory—the children God has given to Him.
He's not ashamed to call us His brethren because
His death made atonement for our sin.

In the days of His flesh, Jesus offered
prayer and tears to the one who could
save Him from death—God on High.
So now the author of our
salvation understands us.
To our weaknesses Jesus can identify.

The Holy Spirit says, "Be faithful to
God; do not harden you hearts
as your fathers did during their wilderness days.
They tested Me; they tried Me; they saw my
works, but they did not know My ways."

From your belief in the living God,
do not depart. Encourage one
another daily, lest you go astray.
For we have become partakers of
Christ if we firmly hold our beginning
confidence to the very last day.

God renews His promise of old that at the
end of our journey we join Him in rest.
Let us keep going, obedient in faith,
as we overcome each earthly test.

God's word is both living and powerful.
As a sword, it cuts to our core.
It discerns our innermost thoughts and
intents; nothing is hidden anymore.

We may think we can cover our sin by
putting on an innocent disguise.
But to God we will give an account; for
all sin is exposed before His eyes.

It is time for you to grow up in Christ,
weaned from "milk" and onto "solid food."
By now, your senses should be exercised so
that you can discern both evil and good.

Those who have professed religion
but still work for their salvation,
will find it impossible to repent of their sin.
For their hearts have been hardened against the
gift of grace, which alone produces faith within.   Matthew 12:32

Do not become sluggish; rather
imitate those who through faith and
patience, the promise will inherit.
When God confirmed His promise
by an immutable oath,
His inability to lie gave it merit.

Jesus is the High Priest of the new covenant—
a priest holy, undefiled, forever perfected.
Once and for all, His sacrifice brings salvation.
Those who come to God through
Him will not be rejected.

Since the first covenant of the
law was found wanting,
God had prepared a more excellent plan.
Not carved on stone or written in a
book, this covenant would be placed
in the hearts and minds of man.

The first covenant had ordinances of
divine service in an earthly sanctuary.
Gifts and sacrifices offered there
were imperfect but necessary.
These temporary sacrifices were symbolic of the
great transformation, which would take place
at the time of God's preplanned reformation.

Now we have a heavenly sanctuary
entered by the spotless Lamb.
Spilling His own precious blood, He redeemed
us from sin before the Great I AM!
He offered Himself once and for all.
For us, He bore sin's degradation.
When He appears again, it will not be for
sin but for our completed salvation!

Let us draw near with a true heart
and a faith that will not waver.
Knowing that He who made these
promises is a faithful Savior.

Faith makes us sure of the
things that we hope for,
and is proof of what we cannot see.
In order for us to receive God's gift of grace,
faith is definitely key!

Faith allows us to believe God is, and if
we seek Him, His reward we will find.
Without faith it is impossible to please our
God; faith is a gift that God has designed.

God approved our forefathers by their faith,
and they are our witnesses even today.
Let us remember their faith in this earthly
life, as they journeyed on their way.

Abel offered a more perfect sacrifice by which
he was declared righteous in spite of his sin.
God rewarded Enoch with eternal life
because he walked with Him.
Noah was warned of things unseen,
and obeyed with Godly fear.
He became an heir of righteousness as
to God's commands he did adhere.
By faith Abraham believed and followed
when he received God's call.
By faith Sarah received strength to conceive.
Through this heir, God would
eventually bless all.

Of these the world was not worthy:
Abraham, Isaac, Jacob, Joseph, Moses,
Rahab and more, Gideon, Barak,
Samson, Jephthah, David, and Samuel—
these who walked in faith before.

The faith of these witnesses can
be our encouragement;
they can be our fans!
They're cheering us on as we continue
the race with all its demands.

Let us lay aside the sin that so easily
ensnares, and be free of its extra weight.
With endurance, let us run following Him
who has promised to set our path straight.   Psalm 5:8

DIANE FRITZ YEO

Keep your focus on Jesus, the one with
whom we started and will finish this race.
For the joy set before Him, Jesus endured the
shame of the cross on which He took our place.
Now He sits on the right hand of
God, offering God's gift of grace.
So compare your trials to what He went through
when you become weary and discouraged too.

The trials you are facing are
part of God's chastening.
For what caring fathers do not
discipline their sons?
So be not discouraged; rather, be encouraged.
Those whom God chastens are His loved ones.
No discipline is joyful for the present.
But after it is through, it should yield the
fruit of righteousness as it was intended to.

Renew your spiritual passion.
Revive those tired limbs!
Avoid any thing that may defile.
Serve God with the reverence due Him.
Continue to offer the sacrifice of praise to
God, always giving thanks to His name.
For yesterday, today, and forever,
our God remains the same!

***

The book of James was written   *James 1–5*
to all the tribes of Israel
who by now had been scattered.
He taught that more than our knowledge and
words, it was our actions that mattered.

James says we can profit from the trials we face if
we allow patience and joy, our fears, to replace.
If you lack wisdom, ask God, believing
His promise to give wisdom is true.
Don't be like waves tossed by the wind,
doubting God will give it to you.
Seek not earthly wisdom but wisdom
from the heavens above.
For that wisdom is pure, peaceable, gentle,
reasonable, impartial, full of mercy and love.

When you are faced with temptations, enticed
by your own desires, do not blame God.
Let your love for Him remain pure.
For it is then that you will be approved
by God and receive the Crown of Life
promised to those who endure.

If you have faith in the saving life
and work of Christ, then yours is a
faith that is alive, not dead.
Living faith produces fruit through works.
All other faith is empty instead.
Actions must follow the truth that you know;
By your works, your true faith
to others you'll show.

Submit to God; resist the devil,
and from you he will flee!
God's Spirit within you will let you know that
you have been set free! Guard your tongue,
for with it you can both bless and curse.
An uncontrolled tongue, not much can be worse!

Show no partiality to those who
enter your assembly door.
Rich oppressors will be judged—
oppressors of the poor.
Be patient and persevering;
judge not one another.
Pray for the sick among you; bring
back your erring brother.

It is good to remember life is a mere vapor; it
appears for a time, and then it vanishes away.
Make your hearts ready, and know
that your plans would be insignificant
if the Lord should return today!

***

Peter echoes words of other writers as   *1 Peter 1–5*
he sends hope and encouragement
to the persecuted Christians of his day.
Note his message of victory through suffering,
triumph over trial in all that he has to say.

You faithful pilgrims of Jesus Christ have
an inheritance that will not fade away.
This saving gospel was revealed by the prophets
yet was meant for us in this present day.

You were once born of the flesh with a
carnal nature, one that was sold to sin.
But now you've been redeemed by Christ's
blood incorruptible, spiritually born again.

You are being kept by the power of God in
your faith, sanctified by the Spirit and sealed.   Ephesians 1:13
May that precious faith being tested by fire
prove to be genuine when Christ is revealed.

You have come to Christ, the Chief
Cornerstone, and by believing in
Him, you will not face shame.
You have become living stones, a
royal priesthood, a chosen nation, as
out of the darkness you came.

Do not fear those who threaten you;
they will give an account to Him.
But be ready to share with those who
question the reason for your hope within.

Rejoice that you can partake of Christ's suffering.
Like Him, you are bringing God glory too.
Elders, shepherd the flock, for they
have been entrusted to you.
Youth, humble yourselves before God.
He will exalt you in due hour.
Resist your adversary, the devil; as
a lion he seeks to devour.

Stand steadfast; in your faith remain true.
Cast your cares upon Him,
knowing He cares for you.

***

Realizing his earthly life will soon　　　　　　　　　　　　　　*2 Peter*
be over, Peter's second letter
emphasizes three things for his
readers to bear in mind.
Three greater reminders for all Christians, both
then and now, would be difficult to find.

Grow in your faith, adding virtue,
knowledge, self-control, perseverance,
godliness, kindness, and love.
All our prophecy comes not from man's will,
but by the inspiration of the Spirit above.
For them is reserved the justice of
God—the blackest, darkest day!

Beware of false prophets and
teachers among you,
seeking to lead you astray.
With deceptive words they will try to exploit
you; do not follow their destructive way.
These false teachers are like wells without
water, clouds carried by a tempest away.

Remember the words spoken to
you by the holy prophets
and us the apostles of the Lord.
For scoffers will come in the last days,
walking in their own lustful ways,
questioning God's promising word.
"Where is this God who you claim is
coming again?" they will say. Remember,
concerning His promise, God is not slack.
A thousand years of our time
is to Him but one day.

God is not willing that anyone perish
but that all might repent.
For the day of the Lord will come as a thief in
the night; the earth and all in it will be spent!
But we as believers look for a new earth
where righteousness dwells, according
to the promises He has said,
Let us be diligent as we wait for His coming,
steadfast in faith, not by error being led!

I have found His great promises forever ring true,
as I claim them as mine in what I seek to do.
Through His promises, of His divine
nature I may partake, escaping the world's
influence in decisions I make.

***

The three Epistles of John were   *1, 2, 3 John*
written by one who has seen,
heard, and touched the Incarnate One.
Through his letters, John emphasizes
the union of believers
with Christ, God's only Son.
Being one in Christ, we as believers will exhibit
righteous behavior, including loving one
another as was commanded by our Savior.

God is light; in Him there is no darkness;
in the light there is no room for sin.
We must confess and be cleansed by Jesus's
blood if we are to find fellowship with Him.

If we say we know Christ, there will be some sign
With His presence in us, our life
to His own He will realign.
It will be our desire to walk as Jesus did, loving
God and our brother, as His commandment said.   John 13:34–35

We cannot love the world.
All the sinful self desires, what we see,
want, and take pride in are of this
world and will come to an end.
But he who wants what God
wants will abide forever.
Eternity with Him we will spend.

Beware of the deceivers of this world who
will come; they will deny Jesus Christ
came in the flesh as God's Son.
These are liars and antichrists who in the
doctrine of Christ do not believe.
Neither greet them nor offer them fellowship;
none of these should you receive.

Remember the truth you heard in the beginning;
be not deceived when the last hour draws near.
Knowing He that is in you is greater
than he in this world should help
you to overcome all your fear.

In God's love He has called us His children,
and if children we are sister and brother.
Let us make ourselves pure just as He is pure.
It is imperative we love one another!
Let us not love in word only but by
providing for a brother in need.
That God loved us and has given us life
through His Son, is the greatest love indeed!

When we pray, we are to pray according to God's
will, as Christ did on that crucifixion day.
Then we can be confident that God's will for us
is good, acceptable, and perfect in every way.   Romans 12:2

***

Jude's book is a letter to those who   *Jude*
have been sanctified in Christ.
He denounces evil and encourages that
for their faith they earnestly contend.
For there are those who have crept in their
fellowship unnoticed—ungodly men, against
whom they must themselves defend.

He warns them that Christ will come
back as promised to execute judgment
because both God and Christ they deny.
Jude gives examples from history of
perverters of truth who already received
punishment from God on High.

Stay in God's love; pray in the Spirit.
Look forward to our Lord's
mercy in the coming days.
To Him who is able to keep you from
stumbling, give all glory, honor, and praise.

***

The final book in the word of God   Revelation
is the book of Revelation.
Of all the prophecies that have
preceded it, it is the culmination.
It is the unveiling of our Lord Jesus Christ—
who He is, was, and forever shall be.
Seated with majesty, crowned with glory,
Christ is clothed with all authority!

There is a special blessing for those who read
or hear what this prophecy has to say.
But there is also a curse on those who from
this book would add or take away.

The apostles had already faced death,
martyrs for preaching their beliefs.
John, still alive, was exiled to Patmos,
an island belonging to Greece.
He was given this revelation in a vision
as he was praying on the Lord's Day.
Behind him, a loud trumpet voice sounded,
and this is what he heard the voice say:
"I am the Alpha and the Omega, the First
and the Last, the Beginning and the End.
All that you see, write in a book; to the
seven churches of Asia this message send."

John turned and saw seven golden lampstands;
among them was the Son of Man.
His head and hair were white as snow,
His eyes, like a burning flame!
His feet were brass and His voice like
the sound of many waters came.
His right hand held seven stars; from His
mouth a two-edged sword extended.
His countenance was like that of the sun.
John fell at His feet as though his life ended!

But the Son of Man reassured John,
saying, "I am He who lives, was dead,
but now lives forevermore.
Write the things that are now, the things you
will see, and the things you have seen before."

He explained that the seven stars are the
messengers to the seven churches, which
are represented by the seven lampstands.
To the believers of the church in
Ephesus, Christ had come and now
held the church's life in His hands.
Christ recalled their good works, the
patience with which they did labor.
But instructed them to repent of their sin, for
they had lost the first love of their Savior.
"You must repent, lest your lamp
stand be removed from its place.
You who overcome will eat of the tree
of life," was His promise of grace.

His message to the church in Smyrna was that
Christ was aware of their difficult situation.
He warned them of continuing persecution
and ten days of tribulation.
But like He Himself, who was dead
but came of life, they need not fear the
second death—eternal separation.
To them, His promise, "You will receive
the crown of life, as you faithfully
face all blasphemy and strife."

Christ warned the church in Pergamos against
associating with the false teachers of their day.
The evil Nicolaitans' and Balaamites' distortion
of God's Word was leading their people astray.
"Repent, or the sword of My mouth
will act as a judge over you!
Overcome, and you'll receive living
manna and a brand-new name too!"

After acknowledging the good
in the church of Thyatira,
Christ warned them against a lack of purity.
There was a leader in the church who was
promoting a lifestyle of immorality.
"I have given them a chance
that they might repent.
But now I come with eyes flaming,
bringing judgment.
To you who have remained pure, hold fast to
good until the end. Overcome, and the gift
of power over nations to you I will send."

To the church in Sardis,
"Your reputation may be that you are fruitful;
but I have seen this is true only in part.
You belong to Christ in name only,
but have not taken Him to heart.
Come, awake, those who are not dead!
Remember what you once heard
and received instead! Repent and
strengthen the good that remains.
Obey, and from the Book of Life,
I will not blot your names!
Overcomers will be clothed in white
garments cleansed from their sin.
Their names will be confessed before
God, worthy only because of Him.

Entrance to the Kingdom of God is in Christ's
hands, for it is He who holds the key.
To the church in Philadelphia, He now
offers an open door of opportunity.
"Because you have persevered, even
though at times your strength is small,
I will make your enemies know I love
you; at your feet in worship they'll fall!
Behold, I am coming quickly! Hold fast to
what you have and the crown that is yours.
To become a pillar in the temple of My God
is my promise for him who endures."

Christ sees the condition of the church
of the Laodiceans: they have become
lukewarm in their devotion to Him,
depending on their own prosperity.
He says, "Because you are not either an extreme
hot or cold, you have become an insult to
Me! Don't you see your true condition is
wretched, miserable, poor, naked and blind?
I counsel you to buy My gold, which
in the fire has been refined.
And be clothed with snow-white garments
that have been provided by Me. Anoint your
eyes with salve that you may be able to see.
In love I ask that you repent and
confess your self-sufficiency!
I am knocking at your heart's door; won't
you hear My voice and allow Me in?
Whoever opens the door, I will enter
and dine together with him.
He who overcomes will share
My throne with Me.
I also overcame; at My Father's right
hand is where I am to be!"

To all the seven churches, lend your ear!
What the Spirit has said, let each one hear!"

Continuing in the Spirit, John was
beckoned to enter a door leading to heaven's
space, that he might be shown things by
the Spirit that yet must take place.
John saw the One resembling jasper and
carnelian who occupied heaven's throne.
Encircling the throne was a rainbow shining
like an emerald, a precious green stone.
Surrounding the throne were twenty-four
elders clothed with robes of pure white.
There were voices and thundering; Seven Spirits
of God and a sea of crystal came into sight.
Four living creatures gave constant
praise, saying, "Holy, holy, holy,
Lord God Almighty, who was
and forever shall be."
In worship, the twenty-four elders
cast their crowns before Him,
falling down on bended knee.
"You are worthy, O Lord; glory,
honor, and power are yours.
for You created all things; by You
each thing exists and endures."

Voices of angels were heard saying, "Worthy is the Lamb who was slain, to receive power and riches, and wisdom, and strength, and honor, and glory, and blessing!"

In the right hand of the One on
the throne was a scroll.
John heard an angel ask who was worthy to
open the scroll and loose the seven seals.
But no one in heaven or earth or
under the earth was able to do so; no
one answered the angel's appeals.

As John wept in sorrow, an elder reassured
him there was One who was able,
One who had prevailed.
The Lion of Judah, the Root of David, the
Lamb was this One who was worthy—
the One who had not failed.
All the creatures and elders fell down
before Him and sang a new song,
"You are worthy to open the scroll, for
You are the Lamb that was slain.
Your shed blood purchased men from
every tribe, tongue, people, and nation,
who no longer in bondage remain!
You have made them to be a kingdom and priests
to serve God; it is on earth that they will reign."

Then suddenly, the elders and creatures
were surrounded by thousands and
thousands of angels—an angelic throng.
"Worthy is the Lamb to receive power,
riches, wisdom, strength, honor, glory
and blessing," was their song.
More voices joined in as every creature
in heaven, earth, and under the earth,
as well as those in the sea, said, "Praise,
honor, power, and glory forever and ever
to God and the Lamb of God be!"
Then the four living creatures said,
"Amen and Amen," as the elders fell
down to honor and worship Him.

Then Christ the Lamb took the scroll
and began to remove each seal.
Events of judgment that would come
to the earth, each one did reveal.
The first was a white horse ridden by
one who will come to conquer the
earth; to him was given a crown.
The second seal brought a rider on a red horse.
With the sword given him, he'd
take the peace down.

The third seal revealed a black horse
whose rider held a pair of scales in his
hand, demonstrating scarcity, inequality,
and famine throughout the land.
As the fifth seal was opened, cries
of martyrs were heard,
"How long until judgment falls on those
who opposed our witness of the word?"
To each one was given a robe of white and the
answer, "A while longer when time is right."
The sixth seal revealed additional judgment
would come; earthquakes and changes
will occur in the stars, moon, and sun.
All rebels will seek safety, realizing that
the wrath of the Lamb has begun.

Before the seventh seal was broken, each of
144,000 from the twelve tribes of Israel was
marked with God's seal on his forehead.
They would be preserved from the wrath of
God, for they were to be His witnesses instead.

Then a multitude joined them—people
from every tribe, tongue, and land.
They were clothed in white robes and
holding palm branches in each hand.
They cried, "Salvation belongs to our God
who sits on the throne and to the Lamb!" An
elder revealed these were those who had come
from the great tribulation, those who had been
washed in the blood of the Lamb. They would
now dwell with and serve day and night
He who sits on the throne—the Great I Am!
They'll no longer hunger nor thirst;
they'll not utter painful cries.
For the Lamb will be their Shepherd;
God will wipe all tears from their eyes.

At the opening of the seventh seal
in the presence of God all of heaven stood still.

The prayers of the saints were laid on the altar.
God would answer these; His
holiness could no longer delay.
The earth must be cleared of its wickedness.
Judgment would continue this day.
Seven angels were given seven trumpets
with which to sound the battle cry.
Each trumpet would bring more judgment upon
an impenitent earth, who still their God deny.
As the first four trumpets sound, judgment
falls on earth's vegetation, its waters,
and light sources from the sky.

As trumpets 5 and 6 sound, Apollyon
leads armies of locusts released
from the bottomless pit.
With stinging tails like that of scorpions,
much torment they will emit!
An army of horsemen numbering two
hundred million from the East will descend.
Who but the Lord Jesus Christ can defeat them?
Only He can bring this battle to an end!

It was revealed to John that the Gentiles will
trample the holy city for forty-two months.
During this time God will send His two
witnesses to preach against the world's sin.
The power God gave to Moses and
Elijah will be given to them again.
When their testimony on earth is through,
by the warring beast they'll be slain.
Their enemies will rejoice for three days,
as in the street their bodies will remain.
Then God will breathe His breath
of life into them once more.
Their terrified enemies will see them rise
to their feet, as alive as ever before!
A voice from the heavens will sound,
causing a shockwave of fear.
The words of instruction to the
witnesses: "Come up here!"
The witnesses on a cloud will
ascend; an earthquake will occur;
seven thousand lives will end!

At the sound of the seventh trumpet,
Satan's earthly rule is constrained.
From loud voices sounding in the
heavens, the kingdoms of our Lord
and of His Christ are proclaimed!

Then God's temple in heaven was opened,
and the ark of the covenant came into view.
Lightning, thunder, an earthquake, and great
hail announced many wondrous signs were due:
A woman appeared who was with
child and about to give birth.
A fiery red dragon who meant to harm the
child hurled one-third of the stars to the earth.
A war in the heavens occurred,
resulting in the dragon's defeat.
He was hurled from the heavens, this
dragon, Satan, author of all deceit.
He sought to kill this child, Jesus, who would be
snatched up to God's throne. Knowing his time
is short, he'd not leave these earthlings alone.
Much persecution the dragon would bring
to the woman (Israel) and to her offspring!

Then John saw a beast with ten horns
and seven heads coming out of the sea.
He spoke proud words and blasphemies
as he exercised his authority.
When he opened his mouth, he blasphemed
God, His name, and all who in heaven dwell.
All those on earth whose names are not in
the Lamb's Book of Life will worship this
antichrist and his leader—the dragon that fell.

A second beast with two horns and the voice
of a dragon was given great power to deceive.
Performing miraculous signs and
wonders, he caused people to believe.
He spoke for the first beast who had
been wounded by a sword.
He forced earth's inhabitants to worship
an image of the first beast as lord.
All who would buy or sell on their forehead
or hand the sign of the beast must fix.
Let anyone who understands
calculate the number of the beast;
it's the number of man: 666.

The Lamb appeared on Mt.
Zion with the 144,000.
As harp music played, they
sang before the throne.
These were the first fruits redeemed
to God and the Lamb.
No one else could sing their song,
for it was theirs alone.

Three angels came next; each
one made a proclamation.
The first preached the gospel to every
tribe, tongue, people, and nation.
"Fear God; judgment is to come;
worship the God of all creation!"

Then from another angel, "Babylon has
fallen; she caused others to drink of the
wine of wrath of her fornication."
The third angel followed with a warning:
"Anyone who worships the beast,
receiving his mark, shall also drink of
the wrath of God's indignation!
They shall be forever tormented in the
presence of the holy angels and the Lamb."
The saints will need to endure, remain
faithful, and keep God's commands.
A voice said, "Blessed are those who die in
the Lord from now on, for they rest from
their labors, but their works follow on."

Then one like the Son of Man came with a
sickle in his hand; on earth it was harvest time!
An angel, also bearing a sickle, joined in
reaping the grapes of wrath from earth's vine.

Then John saw another sign in the heavens:
seven angels bearing the seven last plagues.
With these God's wrath would be complete.
On a sea of glass mingled with fire stood those
whom the beast had had no power to defeat.
With harps in hand, they sang the song
of Moses and the song of the Lamb.
"Great and marvelous are your works,
Lord God Almighty, the Great I Am!
Who shall not fear You and glorify Your name?
All shall worship before You;
Your holiness proclaim!"
God's glory and His power filled
the temple with smoke.
"Go pour out the bowls of wrath on the earth,"
a loud voice spoke.

The first angel tipped his bowl and began to
pour; those who had worshiped the beast,
receiving his sign, were dealt awful sores.
As the second and third bowls were
poured, blood replaced the waters of the
seas, rivers, and fresh springs too.
An angel proclaimed, "Your
judgment is righteous, O God.
Those who have slain Your prophets and
saints have received their just due!"
The fourth bowl was poured on the sun;
extreme heat from the sun was vented.
Yet not one among those who was scorched
called out to God nor repented.
The fifth bowl brought pain and darkness
upon the kingdom of the beast.

But still, they blasphemed the God of
Heaven, not a sign of regret—not the least!
When the sixth angel poured from his
bowl, the great Euphrates was dried up.
A pathway for the Eastern kings it did provide.
To the final battle of God Almighty, the
demons of the dragon, beast, and false
prophet were calling their allies worldwide.

Christ warned, "I come as a
thief comes in the night."
Blessed is he who is watching,
keeping his garments white."

As the seventh bowl was poured, a
voice sounded, "It is done!"
And the earth began to shake.
Cities fell, islands dissolved,
mountains crumbled,
with the force of the mighty earthquake!
From the heavens great hailstones rained
down on an earth so perverse.
Men blasphemed God; this plague
sent by Him, they did curse.

An angel showed John the great
harlot of the earth,
whose doom was now at hand.
For her deception of the world
and shed blood of the saints,
her destruction was God's command.

The apostles and prophets would
be avenged by God
as the great city called Babylon, with all
her wealth, commerce, and power,
would lie in total desolation when
the judgment of God
would bring her to ruin in the
time of just one hour.

In the heavens, John heard a great choir
of voices resounding in praise,
"Alleluia! Salvation, glory, honor, and
power to our Lord God belong!"
As the voice from the throne
encouraged them, a multitude joined
worshiping God with their song:
"Hallelujah! Our Lord God almighty reigns!
Rejoice and be glad; give Him the glory
for the marriage of the Lamb has come!
In fine linen His wife is arrayed.
Blessed are those who to the
Lamb's supper are invited!"
For you, the church, are His bride;
with the Lamb you'll be united!

Next, John saw the heavens opened,
and on a white horse rode the one
called Faithful and True.
With eyes blazing like fire and wearing
many crowns on His head,
He had a name written that no one
except He Himself knew.

The Word of God was dressed
in a robe dipped in blood;
with justice He will judge and make war.
Out of His mouth comes a sword with
which to strike down the nations,
as never has been done before.
With an iron scepter He will rule. The
wrath of the Almighty He brings!
On His robe and thigh is written,
"Lord of Lords and King of Kings."

Armies of heaven, riding white
horses follow after Him.
They are dressed in fine linen, clean and white.
The beast and earth's kings rally their armies
in preparation for their final fight.

But into a lake burning with sulfur were
cast the false prophet and beast.
The armies were killed with His sword;
the birds of the air invited to feast.

John saw an angel from heaven
come bearing a great chain and a key.
To the angel that awful serpent of
old would be forced to submit.
No longer would Satan deceive the nations.
Bound with the chain, he'll be
thrown into the pit!

For one thousand years, Christ and His
resurrected saints will live together and reign.
At the end of this time, Satan will be released,
but his continued rebellion God will contain.
Fire from heaven God will reign down
to crush Satan's final endeavor.
With the beast and false prophet in the
lake of fire, Satan will suffer forever!

John then saw a great white throne, and He
who sat there would judge the wicked dead.
Seeking but not finding a hiding place, they'd
face the Lord Jesus Christ with utmost dread.
By the books they'd be judged
for their every deed.
Their chances ended; they could
no longer be freed.
In the Book of Life, their names
had not been recorded.
Into the lake of fire with death and
Hades, they would be transported.

As we come to the close of the book of Revelation,   *Revelation 21*
we see through John's eyes a
complete transformation.
The sinful earth and heavens
above will no longer exist.
All of sin's evil, sickness, and disease
by God will be dismissed.
With His new creation, God's curse on
the earth will be covered entirely.
And with our Lord and Savior Jesus
Christ, we shall dwell for eternity!

Now John saw a new heaven and a new earth;
the old heavens and earth with
its sea had passed away.
The new Jerusalem came down from the heavens
prepared by God as a bride adorned
for her wedding day.

A loud voice announced that God
would now dwell with man.
They will be His people and He, their God,   Leviticus
according to His promised plan.   26:11–12
"I will wipe away all tears from man's eyes; no
more pain, sorrow, or crying, for no one dies!
All former things have passed away;
behold, I make all things new.

I am the Alpha and Omega, the
Beginning and the End.
Write, for these words are faithful and true.
To him who thirsts, I will give the
fountain of the water of life.
All others will have their part in
the lake of burning fires.
Those who face the second death are
cowardly, unbelieving, immoral, murderers,
sorcerers, idolaters, and liars."

Then an angel carried John away in the Spirit to
a high mountain; the New Jerusalem he'd see.
The holy city descended from the heavens
illuminated only by God's glory.
Its light shone like a most precious
stone, a jasper stone, clear as crystal.
A high wall surrounded the city; on
its twelve pearly gates were written   Ezekiel
the twelve tribes of Israel.   48:31–34

All the city was pure gold, shining clear as glass.
Its streets, too, were paved with gold.
The angel measured the square city.
It was twelve thousand furlongs, John was told.
The wall measured 144 cubits, and
of pure jasper it was made.
In the foundation of its wall,
12 precious stones of all kinds were laid.   Ephesians 2:20
Also in the foundation, each of the 12 apostles
was honored by the writing of his name.
This would definitely be the greatest and
most enduring of all the halls of fame!

All the nations of the saved will
walk in the city's light.
It has no need for a sun or moon,
for there will be no night.   Isaiah 60:20
Nothing impure will enter the city,
neither any deceit nor shame.   Joel 3:17
Only those may enter if in the
Lamb's Book of Life,
God has recorded their name.

John saw the river of life flowing from
the throne through the city street.
The tree of life was on either side,
yielding its fruit so sweet.
Its leaves would be a healing balm; no
longer a curse would there be.
With His name on their foreheads,
God's servants will see His face,
serve, and reign for eternity.

John then hears the words of Jesus,
"Behold, I will come soon!
Blessed is he who understands
this prophecy is true."
John, in awe, fell at the feet of the angel,
offering the worship he felt due.
But the angel replied, "Worship God,
for I am just one like you."

Then Jesus said that the time was
near that He'd reward everyone.
Each would receive a reward
according to what he had done.
"Blessed are those who have washed their robes
and follow My commands,for they have the right
to the tree of life as they enter Jerusalem's gate.
Outside will reside all the evildoers, the
immoral and lovers of pleasure.
For them it will be too late."

Jesus again verified it was He who sent His angel
to justify the churches both near and far.
"I am the Root and the offspring of David,
the Bright and Morning Star."

Then the invitation for the thirsty to
come and partake of the water of life was
offered by both the Spirit and Bride.
And the warning was given to take
seriously and not change
the words that this prophecy does describe.

He who testifies of all these things says,
"Surely I am coming quickly."
Even so, come, Lord Jesus!

Conclusion

There is no reason to fear death or the end of time as the book of Revelation describes, if you do the following:

Admit your need:
- I am a sinner in need of a Savior to reconcile me before God. I cannot save myself.

Believe this truth:
- Jesus is the Christ, the Savior who died for the sins of man and rose from the grave, triumphant over both sin and death.

Ask and receive:
- I ask that you forgive me of my sin and become Lord of my life. Strengthen me with Your Spirit that I might live my life for you.

It is my hope that the abbreviated stories and condensed teaching in this poetic rhyme of the Bible will "whet the reader's appetite" so they will desire to read God's Word in its entirety, asking God to reveal more fully His truth and blessings.

A quote from St. Augustine: "Thou, oh Lord, hast made us for Thyself, and we are restless till we rest in Thee."

Acknowledgments

I want to give special thanks to my husband, Larry, who has always wanted the best for me. His encouragement and support kept me writing. Also, thank you, to my daughter, Molly, who saw value in publishing my poetry and actually began the process for me. Finally, I have been blessed by my granddaughter, Anika, who used her artistic talent to create the illustrations for OMWG. I could mention numerous people who have contributed to my consciousness of God, of myself, and of others during my time here on Earth. Thanks be to God for all of you!

About the Author

Diane is the wife of fifty-six years to Larry Yeo and the mother of a daughter, Molly, and a son, Brennan. She is the grandmother of five.

Having decided as a first grader that she loved learning and teaching, she pursued education as her profession. She received her degree from the University of Sioux Falls and went on to teach elementary children for twenty-five years.

Her love of teaching and her interest in God's Word has led her to many years of leadership in Bible studies in her church, as well as two interdenominational organizations, BSF and CBS.

Working beside her husband, Diane has had an active part in several businesses, including an orchard, a store, a restaurant, and two motels.

Now retired, Diane continues to be involved in a Bible study and enjoys mentoring others. She and Larry reside in Sioux Falls, South Dakota.